THE ART OF HITTING .300

A Mountain Lion Book

E. P. DUTTON   New York

THE ART OF HITTING .300

by Charley Lau with Alfred
Glossbrenner

Revised by Tony LaRussa with Charles Salzberg

Photographs by Leonard Kamsler and Jon Naso

Published in the United States by E. P. Dutton, a division of New American Library, 2 Park
Avenue, New York, N.Y. 10016.

Library of Congress Catalog Number: 85-52464

ISBN: 0-525-24435-2 (cloth)
　　　　0-525-48219-9 (paper)

Published simultaneously in Canada by Fitzhenry & Whiteside Ltd., Toronto

Designed by Nancy Etheredge

10 9 8 7 6 5 4 3 2 1

Second Edition

To my mother and father

for their patience, support, and encouragement

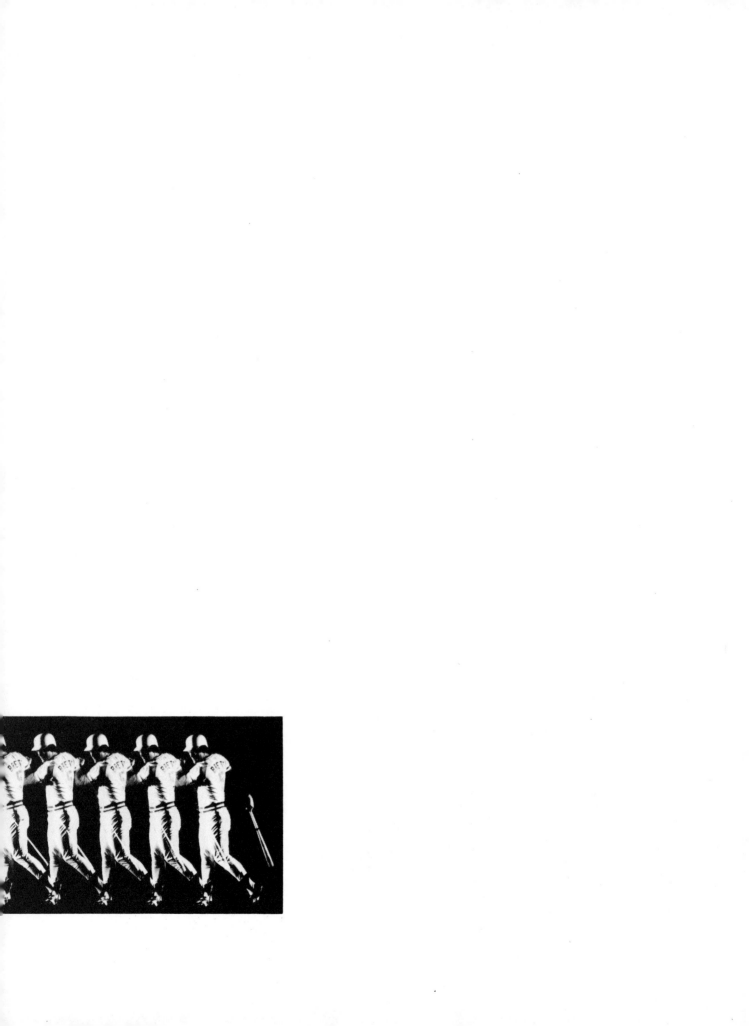

CONTENTS

ACKNOWLEDGMENTS

The authors would like to thank Mickey Morabito, Director of Publicity for the New York Yankees and Pete Sheehy, Yankee Equipment Manager for their help. Also, we would like to thank photographer Leonard Kamsler for his superb stroboscopic, multi-frame, stop-action, and freeze-action shots, Ira Mandelbaum of Scope Associates, and Bruce Brass of Wide World Photos for his assistance with the hitter analysis photos. We'd also like to thank George Brett for his patience, for his fine hitting, and for being such an all around nice guy.

THE ART OF HITTING .300

1
THE MOST DIFFICULT CHALLENGE

Hitting a baseball has been called the most difficult feat in all sports. There's a lot of truth in that statement, yet I don't think I'd put it quite that way. Not that hitting is ever easy. It's just that I think you could probably swing blindfolded and manage to hit the ball every once in a while. The *real* challenge, the thing that can keep ballplayers awake nights, is to hit the ball *consistently*—day after day, in game after game throughout the season. This is so tough, so demanding, that there just isn't any doubt in my mind that it's the hardest thing to do in baseball. And I wouldn't be surprised if hitting consistently turned out to be the most difficult feat in *all* sports.

It's consistency that sets a good hitter off from someone who's just average or downright poor. And the need to maintain consistency can make even players who regularly bat around .300, the traditionally accepted mark of excellence, feel insecure. All major-league players, regardless of how much they're paid or how many millions of fans idolize them, are constantly aware that no matter how well they do today, they'll have to prove themselves all over again tomorrow and the next day, and the next day, and the day after that.

These are men who hit for a living, and as a group they represent the best baseball players in the country. But players of all levels of ability and at all levels of competition face exactly the same problem. The pressures may not be as intense, and the games less frequent, but the task is just as great. Every player at every level knows that no matter what he does, he'll never reach a point where he feels totally secure, where he can honestly say that he doesn't worry about whether he'll be able to hit the ball or not.

MAKING IT EXTRA TOUGH

To make things worse, once you're hitting pretty well and get to be known around your league, opposing pitchers begin to really bear down on you. All of a sudden you represent a threat. The pitchers know you can beat them. They know they've got to be especially careful when you're at the plate. So they study your weaknesses and really hump up against you, making things a lot tougher than they otherwise would.

It seems to me that this is even truer today than in the past. Years ago, for example, whenever the count was 2–0 or 3–1, a batter could usually expect the next pitch to be a fast-ball strike. Since the pitcher was behind, he'd figure he had to take a chance. If you hit the ball, he could always hope his teammates would catch it or put you out. If you didn't hit it, he'd have another strike on you.

It was a chance many pitchers felt was worth taking, and the 2–0 or 3–1 fast ball became a rule of thumb. You can see the effect of this approach by checking the box scores of games played twenty or thirty years ago. You'll notice a lot of thirteen-hit shutouts, something that you don't run into very often today.

I don't know just why this is. It could be because of new techniques, the increased importance of the home run, or just a new philosophy of pitching. But whatever the reasons, today a good hitter can no longer count on a fast ball in a 2–0 or 3–1 situation. The pitcher is more likely to forget about putting the next ball down the pipe for an assured strike and concentrate instead on nipping the inside or outside corner of the plate, where a strike is less certain. This is especially true if you've got a reputation as a good hitter, and it makes your job that much harder.

CONTACT FIRST, HOME RUNS LATER

Pitchers, though, are only one of the forces working against a batter. Another very strong, and I think negative, influence is the dominance of the home run as possibly the most desirable play in baseball. Everybody wants to hit home runs, and a lot of players are so home-run-conscious that they try to hit one each and every time they come up to bat. This would be fine, were it not for the fact that by trying to hit a home run every time they do themselves and their teams a lot of damage. If they would just try to hit the ball, they and their clubs would be much better off.

Don't get me wrong. There's no question that the home run can be one of the most valuable and spectacular plays in baseball. I get as excited as anyone else when one of our guys knocks one out of the park, particularly if it comes at a crucial moment in a game. And I think anyone who can hit twenty or thirty home runs a season in the majors deserves to be admired for the combination of talent and skill needed to make that possible. What's more, I feel that to be a truly complete hitter, you've got to be able to pull the ball for the home run when the situation demands it.

However, what everyone seems to overlook is that home-run hitting is a special technique calling for *advanced* skills. It is not something a player should try to do from the start and certainly not something he should make his only goal. It's much more important to develop good mechanics and master the skill of making contact with the ball first. Later, if you discover you have a talent for it, by all means go on to master the technique of home-run hitting.

When you approach hitting this way, you'll not only improve your average, you'll find that the same good mechanics you've developed to make consistent contact will make you a much better home-run hitter as well. Good mechanics, in other words, will make you a winner.

HOW HOMERS CAN HURT YOU

At the same time, though, it's important to realize that just as everyone who plays the guitar can't expect to become a rock superstar, not everyone who can hit is cut out to be a home-run hitter. And generally, players who force themselves in that direction when hitting home runs is not one of their talents cause themselves nothing but grief. But then, it isn't always the individual who does the forcing. Sometimes it's the team management.

As I've traveled this country giving talks and clinics in various places, I've had a chance to meet lots of Little League, high school, college, and other coaches and managers. Without exception I've found them to be fine, dedicated people who want nothing but the best for the boys on their teams. But, like most major-league coaches, they also want big, strong home-run hitters—someone who can pull the ball and send it sailing over the right- or left-field fence. That's what they work on and what they stress. And while you can hardly blame them for thinking that way, that's also where the trouble begins.

The problem is that if every time you come up to bat you're looking to belt one out of the park, you're not going to be able to hit consistently. To pull the ball and hit home runs, your bat head has got to meet the ball at least two feet out in front of the plate—which means you've got to be exceptionally quick. Your bat head must travel a greater distance to meet the ball out there and it's got to get there sooner than with any other kind of hit. In addition, since bat and ball must come together in one small area, you have almost no margin for error. This is why pull hitters are rarely consistent hitters. They either hit it or they miss it completely.

It's an all-or-nothing proposition. By trying to hit the ball so far out in front of the plate, a pull hitter automatically eliminates any possibility of making contact closer in. His bat speed, his timing, and his whole body are geared to hit the ball at the earliest possible moment. Once he's committed, there's no way he can hit the ball at any other point.

Of course, if everything works just right, the results can be impressive. But even if you have a talent for home-run hitting, you can't always count on everything coming together in an ideal way. That's why players who swing hard and try to pull tend to strike out—a lot.

Your chances of getting a hit are much better if you meet the ball some place between two feet in front of the plate and directly above it. Your margin for error is much greater. You don't have to rush, and you can be more selective about what you swing at. You can also be more consistent. Compare this with the gamble involved in trying to pull the ball for a home run and taking a chance on ending up with nothing but a strikeout.

There *are* times when you have to take that gamble. But if you do it every at-bat, you're almost sure to ruin your average and destroy your chances for hitting consistently, which can significantly reduce your value to the team. Yet this is something even major-league team management doesn't always understand. I remember one young player, for example, who was what I considered a superb hitting prospect. This boy had all the marks of a winner. He had the power. He had the stroke. He learned quickly, and he had a good eye.

I worked with him in spring training one year and put all of those points and more in my evaluation report. I also went on record saying that the only thing that would hurt the boy would be if management expected him to hit home runs. I knew, and the player knew, that at that early stage of his career, when he was so young, he wasn't a home-run hitter.

Unfortunately, that's exactly what management expected him to do. Every time he hit the ball to the left of second base or any place other than down the right side, he got yelled at. As a result, he ended up playing Triple-A ball and batting a miserable .193.

I consider that a tragic waste of young talent. But similar things happen at all levels of competition and far more frequently than most people imagine.

WHAT'S IT WORTH?

I've never made a secret of how I feel about this. I've always been an advocate of using the whole field to hit in, of developing a batter's ability to consistently hit the ball to the spot that will do the opposing team the most damage in a given situation. I believe that 99 percent of the time a good hitter should concentrate on hitting, and if he happens to accidentally hit a home run in the process, so much the better.

Consequently, I've been tagged at one time or another as a "Punch and Judy." In the home-run-conscious world of professional baseball, where "just" hitting line drives is sometimes looked down upon, these are not what you'd call complimentary terms. But, while it's a little discouraging to have people forget that I also advocate home-run hitting when the situation demands it, it doesn't really bother me, because I know I've got the numbers on my side. I know that statistically a player who can hit consistently, day after day, is going to produce better results for his team over a season than someone who puts all his effort into hitting home runs. It's as simple as that.

Suppose, for example, that you've got two players on the same team: One guy drives in one run a game for six games, while the other guy hits two home runs with the bases loaded, scoring eight runs. To make the comparison even more dramatic, let's say that the first player doesn't even get a hit. He never gets on base. But he *does* make consistent contact. He hits a sacrifice fly to drive in a man on third when there are less than two out. Or with runners on first and third, he hits the ball to the second baseman's left to both score the man on third and eliminate the double play. Or whatever. The point is that he drives in the runs, even without hitting safely himself. The second player, on the other hand, hits both homers in the best of all possible situations—that is, with the bases loaded.

Now, which player is more valuable to his team? Which is more likely to help his club win the ball games it plays that week?

Naturally, the answer depends upon *when* each player drove in his runs. It's quite possible that in any given week the home-run hitter's performance would be more crucial than the other player's. But over the long haul you've got to believe the other guy's going to be more valuable.

After all, the consistent hitter, the winning hitter, helps produce a run in six different games, while the home-run hitter connects in only two games, striking out in all other at bats. And a lot of the homers he hits over the course of the season are going to come when the score is something like 13–1 or 10–2. If you're behind, a home run can help you catch up in those situations, and if you're ahead it can help make your lead more secure. But more often than not, it's going to be the steady, consistent hitter who contributes more to the margin of victory game after game. This is true whether you play six or seven games a week, as in the majors, a twenty-game college schedule, or some other schedule at another level of the game.

What's more, there are times when going for the home run can involve a big but unnecessary risk. Suppose you're down a couple of runs. You've got runners on second and third, with no outs. What should the next batter do to benefit his club the most?

Whether he bats right- or left-handed, the winning hitter will try to hit the ball to the right of the infield. If he gets on base himself, so much the better. But even if he fails to get a hit, even if he knocks a ground ball right to the second baseman, he will still score the man on third and advance the runner on second to third base. By channeling the ball in that direction, at the very least he'll succeed in exchanging an out for a run and a one-base advance. When the next man comes up, there'll be a runner on third all set to be batted in.

But what if that first batter decides to try for a home run? It's true that it would be a spectacular play if he makes it. But what if he doesn't? What if in his efforts to be a hero he strikes out or pops up or, if he's a right-hand hitter, fails to pull the ball far enough and ends up putting it in the left side of the infield?

He might score the runner with a ground ball to shortstop, but he won't do it with a ground ball to third base. Besides, if he hits it to the shortstop, the runner on second can't advance to third because the play will be right in front of him.

A left-hand hitter might fare better since he's trying to pull the ball to the right. But your chances of making out are increased any time you deliberately try to hit a home run. By trying to be a hero in a situation like this, a player risks leaving his team in exactly the same field position, while costing it an out and reducing the possibility of driving in both runners on second and third.

THE "HERO COMPLEX" VS. ADVANCING THE RUNNER

Yet many a professional ballplayer who by rights ought to know better has taken just that risk, and lost. It's the "hero complex" and it exists in any league. But since it's rooted in the player's ego and since pro ballplayers probably *need* bigger egos than most if they're to be successful, you see it often in the major leagues. The praise and glory that a home run generates can make hitting one an irresistible goal for some players, even though such rewards are usually way out of line with its value to the game and even though a player may have to sacrifice consistency along the way.

Consistent hitters, on the other hand, sometimes aren't even recognized, let alone rewarded for their efforts. That's why I think baseball should have another statistic, one that would recognize the value of consistency by pegging it to its major result: advancing the runner.

Don't forget: A player's batting average gives you only one piece of information. It tells you what percent of his at-bats have resulted in hits. It does not tell you *when* those hits were made or whether they did any good. The same thing's true of the statistics for homers and RBIs.

I think Lee May, Baltimore's hard-hitting first baseman, said it best when he pointed out that he could hit well in only one month, coast the other five months of the season, and *still* generate a respectable number of home runs and RBIs and a batting average of .240 or .250. Lee's point is the same as mine: You could see those stats next to a player's name and still have no idea whether he was a good hitter or not.

A statistic recording "Runners Advanced" would give you a much truer picture of the player's skill as a batter. It could be limited to advancing a runner from first to third, since that hurts the opposing team the most, or it could include other advances as well. Why should a player who is awarded an RBI for bringing a run in from third be the only one to be recognized? Surely the batter who previously advanced the runner to third and thus set up the RBI deserves equal recognition for his contribution to the play.

Obviously, the greater the number of "Runners Advanced," the better. And just as obviously, the only way to rack up impressive statistics in this area would be to hit the ball consistently throughout the season. Being hot for one month just wouldn't do it.

I have no idea whether such a stat will ever be adopted. And there's no way of knowing exactly what effect it would have. But I've got to believe that it would do some good. There are a lot of players who aren't home-run hitters but who nevertheless work hard and make the most of what they have. And there are a lot more who could boost their averages by forty or fifty points if they'd just concentrate on hitting and let the home runs take care of themselves. A statistic like "Runners Advanced" would at least make consistency more rewarding and highlight the accomplishments of those who achieve it, the winning hitters who form the backbone of any contending ball club, manufacturing runs day after day and providing the competitive edge to win the games leading to a league championship.

And consistent hitting *is* an accomplishment, for a number of reasons. In the first place, the plain physics or scientific aspects of the problem make it very difficult. There you are at the plate using a round bat against a round ball and trying to hit the thing squarely. What's more, the ball's coming toward you at around eighty or ninety miles per hour, and it's being directed by someone whose chief goal is to make it impossible for you to hit. You've got pitchers who have learned to spit on the ball, to make it sink or suddenly rise, to make it slide or curve away from you, and to do many other things calculated to make your job harder.

Yet challenging as they are, given a little talent, these problems can be solved. You can learn to hit the ball and hit it with good consistency in spite of the best efforts of most pitchers. It's not easy, but you can do it.

If you avoid the "hero complex" and the emotions that come with it. A lot of individuals can't do this. For them, just hitting the ball isn't enough. They decide that they won't be satisfied unless they hit home runs or pull the ball. Whenever this happens, it inevitably causes the batter to get tense. He begins to put himself under pressure, loses his concentration, and his swing falls apart. Pretty soon he can't hit *anything*, let alone a home run.

You know, I think that if you could take a major-league player of average talent, remove all emotion and ego, and say, "Just hit the ball," he'd probably hit .300. In fact, I can virtually *guarantee* it.

Let's say, for example, that you're that player. You've just been called up from the minors where you've had some success playing Triple-A ball. So you've got some ability. But as yet you have no at-bats in the majors. If you came to me and said, "Charley, what can I do to hit .300?" I could easily tell you. I'd simply say, "If you will try 100 percent of the time—every pitch, every at-bat—to hit the pitcher right in the forehead, you'll hit .300."

That's really all there is to it. By using the pitcher's forehead as a focal point, as a way of channeling your thoughts and energy, you *will* hit the ball. You won't ever go zero for eight; you'll always average one hit a ball game; and you'll get your share of home runs, too.

I realize that sounds extreme, and maybe it is a little exaggerated. But not by much. The few times you miss getting a hit a game, you'll make up for with the two or three hits you get in some other game. By channeling your efforts toward one spot, your mechanics will become good, you'll consistently *average* at least one hit a game, and you'll come damn close to batting .300.

The trouble is, you can't do it. Or, more correctly, you *won't* do it. It's too simple. Human nature being what it is, a man's ego enters the picture and he decides that hitting "just" .300 isn't dramatic enough. It may win ball games, and it may produce a steady flow of runs, but it doesn't necessarily bring the fans to their feet cheering and shouting his name. So he begins to try for home runs, and before you know it, his average begins to drop.

A player's ego and emotion—the "hero complex"—and the tension they create can make hitting twice as difficult as it really is. The batter becomes his own worst enemy. Others don't create the tension—*he* does. And that's the biggest single mistake a batter can make in any league.

A "NATURAL" HITTER?

Another serious mistake that a lot of amateurs and a surprising number of professionals make concerns their mental attitude. I'm talking about the guy who doesn't have very high expectations for himself because he's convinced he's not a "natural" hitter or because he doesn't have the necessary physical attributes. A guy like that usually doesn't try very hard. He says, "What's the use? I'll never be any good anyway." Well, about the politest thing I can say to that is "Baloney!"

Now, I'm not saying that you don't have to have some ability. But that phrase "a 'natural' hitter" is seriously overworked. People look at a guy who hits consistently and maybe even makes it look easy and just assume that he must have been born with the ability to hit a baseball.

Well, maybe so. But I think it's far more likely that he was born with the same abilities most of us are but just developed them better.

Nor is there anything special about a good hitter's physical attributes. "Natural" hitters come in all shapes and sizes. They may have built up their bodies with weights and the proper exercise, but they don't necessarily have any physical trait or traits in common. What they do share is an unswerving determination to make the most of what they have.

And they share something else, too. All "natural" hitters use the same mechanical techniques to put the bat head on the ball. It's this collection of techniques that makes them "natural" hitters, not some accident of birth. And these techniques can be learned by virtually anybody with the desire to improve and a normal amount of hand-eye coordination.

Not everyone agrees with this, and I'd be less than fair if I didn't give them their due. Some baseball coaches and professionals are against what they call "overteaching." They feel that it's wrong to "cloud a player's mind" with instructions and believe that if left alone a hitter will adjust somewhere along the way and more or less learn by himself. I don't agree with this approach, and I guard against it. Yet I do recognize that it can be done, and I've even seen it work with a few players.

But I've also seen players with poor averages improve dramatically simply by concentrating on the techniques used by "natural" hitters. These were players who had been left alone and had *not* learned by themselves. What's more, they had been playing long enough that it was clear they never were going to learn unless somebody taught them. They had ability; they had the desire to improve. All they needed was to be shown what to do.

As far as I'm concerned, showing a player what to do is just common sense. Analyzing what makes a good hitter good, distilling it down to several essential points, and applying it to improve your own hitting is the only logical way to do things. If it didn't work, the critics who fear over-teaching and clouded minds might have a case. But it *does* work. I've *seen* it work. And I can show you how to make it work for *you*.

HITTER ANALYSIS

ROD CAREW
HEIGHT: 6 feet
WEIGHT: 170 pounds
AVERAGE (1985): .280

This picture could be labeled "Artist at Work," for that's exactly what Rod Carew is. There's no tension in this man. He has a great weight shift and a fluid, graceful swing that, as you can see, results in full arm extension even though he doesn't take his top hand off. Rod Carew simply tries to hit the ball, and that fact, plus a lot of talent, has made him possibly the best percentage hitter to come along in the past ten years.

What's more, there's no finer bunter in baseball. Using the same good mechanics of getting to his front leg, shifting his weight, and keeping his eye on the ball, Carew typically gets about thirty bunt base hits a year, which makes him extraordinarily difficult to defense effectively. Aware of his ability to bunt, the third baseman's got to play down his throat, and whenever he comes up, everybody's got to short up a bit—just in case. But playing him in can be a mistake because he's just as capable of putting one into the outfield.

And there he has another remarkable talent. Gene Mauch once told me that he'd never seen another man hit the ball just out of the reach of the fielders with such uncanny frequency. And you know, he's right. Whenever I'd see Carew hit a ball that a fielder missed by just inches, I used to think, "Aw, the lucky so-and-so." But since Mauch said what he did, I started noticing. I don't know how Rod Carew does it, but based on what I've seen, I think Gene Mauch is right.

I also think Carew has another ability. I'm not sure it's deliberate, but if you ever play him and you've got a defensive weakness in the field— some player who may not be as capable as others—*that's* where the ball always seems to end up. Carew will send him a ball that a better fielder would have caught. But when the weaker fielder tries for it he slips or misjudges it and the ball drops in for a base hit.

Rod Carew is an amazing hitter. His skills earned him a .332 average and his first American League batting championship in 1969. He repeated in 1972 with .318, in '73 (.350), in '74 (.364), and in '75 (.359). In 1976, George Brett took the award with a .333 average. But Carew was back in '77 (.388) and in '78 (.333).

Clearly the man has tremendous ability. But without taking anything away from his natural talents, in the end I think it all comes down to one thing: Rod Carew simply makes solid contact with the ball more often than other hitters.

HITTER ANALYSIS

PETE ROSE
HEIGHT: 5 feet, 11 inches
WEIGHT: 192 pounds
AVERAGE (1985): .264

I know there are those who will disagree, but I was very happy when Pete Rose began to make the kind of money he's making now. Rose is a good, solid, consistent line-drive hitter. And that kind of play is so important to the game of baseball that it's only right that it should be rewarded. The home run is important and often necessary. But without the consistent hitting provided by players like Pete Rose, all the home-run hitters in the world couldn't win ball games.

Rose's accomplishment is all the more remarkable when you consider his ability. He's got talent, but left to itself his talent alone would probably not have propelled him to what some people call "superstar" status. And that's precisely the point. Pete didn't just leave his talent to itself. He worked and he worked hard. And because of his tremendous drive and dedication he was able to become a superstar type anyway.

Rose uses the whole field to hit in, and I think his mechanics are basically sound. However, he does bend a lot at the waist in his preparatory stance. As with Stan Musial, this exaggerated crouch isn't necessarily bad in itself, but with Pete I think it can cause him to stick his butt out and put his weight on his heels instead of on his toes. I'm not sure he's always well balanced in his stance.

The picture here shows him just after he's taken his stride. A split second later you'd see a powerful weight shift typical of a big, strong guy used to getting the most out of his body. That, as you can imagine, requires good concentration, and Pete's concentration is total. When taking a pitch he'll follow the ball all the way into the catcher's glove.

And when he faces a pitcher he just never gives up. In fact, it's Pete Rose's ability to fight, fight, fight to hit the ball that sticks out most in my mind. It's an attitude I'd recommend to anybody.

HITTER ANALYSIS

CARL YASTRZEMSKI
HEIGHT: 5 feet, 11 inches
WEIGHT: 175 pounds
AVERAGE (lifetime): .285

Carl Yastrzemski is the only man I've ever seen who was successful starting with the bat held both high and vertical and with it in a wrapped or cocked-toward-the-pitcher position. He's the only player I've ever known who could take an upward hitch and still hit the ball consistently. The answer lies, I think, in the fact that he has an awful lot of ability.

This picture was taken in 1970, and as every Boston fan can tell you, Yaz has modified his stance since then. He now bends much more at the waist, and the bat, though still fairly vertical, is held lower. I think these modifications have probably helped. But his bat still has to make a big arc to get to the ball; consequently Carl still has to commit sooner than players with a shorter, more compact swing.

Yastrzemski is possibly the hardest-working hitter I've ever seen. Boston has traditionally been an offensive club, and I think they may practice hitting longer and harder than any other organization in either league. They have exceptionally good work habits. If they come to your town for a three-game series, I daresay that every day there'd be three guys out on the field hitting early, before the regular batting practice begins. And knowing what a dedicated, hard-working player Carl Yastrzemski is, I wouldn't find it hard to believe that he's taken more batting practice than any other man in the history of the game.

Yet, although it's all related, what I really want to stress is something else. Young fans may not remember it, but Carl Yastrzemski is a guy who couldn't pull the ball the first four years he played. But he was still very successful as a hitter. I've said elsewhere that teams send scouts out through the country trying to find players who can pull the ball and then turn around and try to teach them to make contact and hit the ball the other way.

Well, Yastrzemski was just the opposite. He hit the ball, and he hit it hard. But, primarily because of the hitch up and the big, long arc it created in his swing, he couldn't pull. It was only when he was older and more mature, *after* he was successful, that he learned to pull the ball. And that, I think, is the way it *should* be.

Pulling the ball is an advanced technique. It's important and you should learn to do it if you can, but not *before* you learn to make contact. Let yourself be successful. Let yourself just hit the ball, regardless of where it goes. Then as you mature and get a little smarter and maybe a little stronger, you can always learn to pull. But, like Carl Yastrzemski, learn to make contact and to hit the ball well first.

2
THE "ABSOLUTES" OF GOOD HITTING

I wasn't always aware that "natural" hitters had so much in common. But I've been blessed with an analytical mind, and as a player I probably questioned things more than most. In fact, as a catcher, it was part of my job to know what the opposing batters could and could not hit. From there it was a logical step to ask why some guys were good and others weren't.

Crouching behind the plate, I had a unique vantage point. I was closer to the batter than anyone else and was able to watch every move he made. If he was tense or relaxed, confident or frightened, if he kept moving all the time or stood like a statue, I was aware of it, probably even before his own coach was.

Naturally, I'd use those observations to try to defeat the man. I'd call for pitches calculated to take advantage of any perceived weaknesses. But I would also match up my observations with the batter's performance. And gradually some ideas began to form. Some, as it turns out, were right and some were wrong, but it was a beginning.

As I look back, I think the first guy I really analyzed was my Baltimore teammate Brooks Robinson. I used to squeeze rubber balls and lift weights to build up my wrists and arms, so I was pretty well muscled. But here was Brooks with wrists thinner than I've seen on some women, and he could hit the ball farther than I could. Something like that has just got to make you wonder why.

So I watched Brooks carefully. I saw the way he moved, how he handled the bat, and how he used his body. What I discovered was that Brooks had a certain rhythm and grace, and what I've since learned are excellent mechanics. These qualities helped him get the most out of what he had, and they allowed him to overcome any lack of muscular development.

Mechanics seemed to be the answer I was looking for when analyzing other good hitters as well. And over the next couple of years, recovering from a tendon operation, playing for Atlanta, and managing that organization's Double-A club, I kept focusing on mechanics and getting deeper into the subject. As time went on, the evidence kept mounting to support the idea that all good hitters have certain techniques or moves in common.

When Baltimore hired me as a hitting coach in 1969 and assigned me Mark Belanger as a special project, I had some pretty clear ideas about what makes a good hitter good. But I also knew enough to be aware of how much I didn't know. I didn't let on, of course, and as it turned out Mark and I more or less learned together. I'd try out different ideas and we'd experiment with this or that. That year Belanger had the best batting average he's ever had, so I knew I was on the right track.

Before long Boog Powell, Davey Johnson, and others began to get interested and join our practice sessions, and things just grew. I think almost everybody benefited, for I've found that getting people to think about and analyze their swings is half the battle. It's the first big step toward improvement.

The same thing happened at Oakland in 1970, where Dave Duncan was my special project. We'd work on hitting after the club's main practice, and a number of players would usually stick around to watch. One day Joe Rudi asked if he could join us. I said, "Sure, come on," and a short time later other guys began to take an interest as well. And again things grew.

GETTING IT ALL TOGETHER

In any profession you'll always find people who want to improve, and baseball is no exception. But baseball's different in one major respect. Unlike other professions, baseball has no mechanism, no organized way of collecting and distributing information that may be of value to players. The same is true at the Little League, high school, or college level. So what we're left with are coaches (good, bad, and mediocre) and rules of thumb, some of which work and some of which are dead wrong.

For a lot of players and coaches at all levels, this isn't nearly good enough. Consequently a lot of people are searching, looking for the right answers, for an approach that works. By pulling together a number of things, some of which have been around for years and some of which were based on my own observations, I was able to offer some answers. Because my recommendations were logical, but above all because they worked, people began to listen.

One man who took a particular interest was Ewing Kauffman, owner of the Kansas City Royals. And for a particular reason. In 1971 I was working for the Kansas City organization, and Ewing needed a hitting coach for the baseball academy he had established in Sarasota, Florida.

The idea behind the academy was to systematically train young athletes in baseball fundamentals by putting them through a rigorous program designed to sharpen their skills, develop their talents, and hopefully produce a number of players with major-league potential. It was a great idea, and it was generously funded by Ewing Kauffman. But as with all new and experimental programs, things didn't work out exactly as planned.

Most of the kids were chosen on the basis of their running speed, eyesight, and balance. As a result we ended up with what seemed like every high school and college left halfback in the country. A lot of these kids were fine football players, but they couldn't throw a baseball to save their lives and they couldn't hit even the easiest pitches.

The academy lasted for a few years, and it did produce a few major-league players. But unfortunately, the economy took a nosedive before the academy could really hit its stride, and it had to be shut down. Still, it was an excellent experience for me personally, and it led to something of a breakthrough in my search for the essence of good hitting.

Ewing Kauffman had provided the academy with some of the best videotape and film equipment available. At that time using videotape as a training/teaching device was considered almost revolutionary in some circles. It was a new and highly effective technique, and I made the most of it.

Before going down to Sarasota I could tell a good swing from a bad one with the naked eye and I had some theories. But I still wasn't sure exactly *why* a particular swing was good or bad. At the academy I learned to analyze tape and film. I lived with that VTR machine for close to three years, watching, replaying, and slowing down hundreds of swings.

It wasn't long before I began to see things that are virtually invisible in real time, they happen so fast. Today, since I know what to look for, I can walk by a three-diamond practice field, catch each batter out of the corner of my eye, and without deliberately thinking about it, tell what each is doing right or wrong. But at the time, what I saw on tape and film came as a revelation.

I already knew, for example, that it was important to keep moving in the batter's box. But I wasn't sure of all the alternatives or of what worked and what didn't work. By studying the tapes and running them in slow motion, I could see how crucial body rhythm and the weight shift it made possible were to a good swing. I learned that you've got to go back to be able to go forward. And I discovered that many of the old standby rules of thumb that players have followed for years are completely wrong.

TWO WRONG "RULES"

One such rule concerned which leg you hit from. For years textbooks and coaches have been telling players that "you hit off your back leg"—that is, that your back leg should be your main support when you make contact with the ball. This might be the worst rule ever taught about how to hit, and it's done more to hurt whole generations of hitters than anything else I can name. The rule is not only incorrect, it's also dead wrong. It urges you to do exactly the opposite of what you must do to be a good hitter.

Another "rule" that can do a lot of damage is the one about your top hand. From the time I began playing ball, I'd hear, "top hand, top hand," which is a short way of saying that at the point of contact with the ball you should roll your top hand over. The intent, I suppose, was to help the batter get on top of the ball. But the result was often an artificially shortened, and therefore weakened, swing. Rolling your top hand can make it impossible to get the full extension of your arms so necessary to good hitting.

Now, I'd be the first person to recommend keeping both hands on the bat—*if* you can do it and still get extended. A lot of major-league players are able to do this, and their success is proof that the top-hand rule can work. But there are a lot who can't, and their top hands cause them a lot of trouble.

I don't think it's correct to say that the top hand *has* to come off each time you swing. But at the same time I don't think it's wise to blindly follow the top-hand rule without giving any thought to your arm extension. This is why it can often be a good idea to work on taking the top hand off in practice, even if you keep both hands on the bat during the game. This way you'll be thinking "extension" and be more inclined to get your arms out than someone who hasn't practiced taking his top hand off.

The problems that the top-hand rule can cause some players were especially evident at the Sarasota academy. As I mentioned, we had a lot of former football players there who couldn't hit worth a damn. In addition to an acute lack of baseball experience, they were also hampered by a lack of flexibility. When they'd swing, some of them couldn't move their arms without also moving their heads and entire bodies almost as a single unit. Most of them would try to muscle the ball, using their top hands to apply the force. The results, of course, were not good. But seeing such an extreme example of the problems caused by "top hand" in a bad swing made me even more aware of the subtle influences of the "rule" in a good swing.

At Sarasota I also discovered how critical it is to watch the ball when you hit it. We've all heard the old saying, "Keep your eye on the ball," but I'll bet most people don't know what it really means or how absolutely vital it is to successful hitting. I'd hear that as a player, and I'd do what I thought amounted to keeping my eye on the ball. But as a swinger in any sport—golf, tennis, squash, or whatever—you can never know exactly what you yourself do when you hit the ball. That's why there are coaches, pros, and instructors.

As it happened, I really didn't know what keeping your eye on the ball meant. It was only by feeding balls into a throwing machine and watching hour after hour as different players took batting practice that I discovered the true meaning of "seeing the ball." I just wish I had known it earlier in my career, for I'd have been a much better hitter.

THE ABSOLUTES

These are only a few of the things I've learned about hitting after years of questioning, analyzing, observing, and what I guess you'd call pretty intense study. Yet even after all that time, I'm still learning. I don't ever expect to know all there is to know about hitting.

By now, however, all of the major points are clear. These points are the techniques that all good hitters have in common. They are supported by hundreds of miles of film and tape, thousands of action photos, and considerable testing under fire. I've seen them be effective with so many players that there's no doubt about it: They work.

What's more, they always *have* worked, from the time Abner Doubleday laid out the first baseball diamond right on up to today. For years we've seen good hitters remove their top hands after hitting the ball. We've seen their rhythm and weight shift. And we've seen the top ten hitters in both leagues using the whole field to hit in. It's just that few people have recognized these and other techniques for what they truly are—the *Absolutes* of good hitting.

To hit a baseball consistently, there are certain things you absolutely must do. Some of them may surprise you; some may be contrary to what you've been taught; and some you may have heard previously. In fact, depending upon how much you've played, you've almost certainly run into one or two of the Absolutes before. That's because, as I mentioned earlier, hitting has always been something of a gray area with very little systematic analysis and communication.

One player will discover a technique that works for him while another player someplace else discovers some other techniques. These things get passed along from one guy to the next so that you've got a lot of players with one or more pieces of the puzzle but only a few who have the whole thing put together. Those few are your top hitters in each league. But even they may not know exactly what they do and why it helps them hit.

The Absolutes are the whole puzzle. I'll go into greater detail on each of them and show you how each applies as we work through the swing in the following chapters. But for now take a look at this list and the brief explanations of each technique. As you'll see later, the Absolutes really are like pieces in a puzzle, for they're all connected with each other in one or more ways. Because of this it's important to have the whole picture in mind before getting into specifics.

THE ABSOLUTES OF GOOD HITTING

1. *A balanced, workable stance.* All good athletes are balanced most of the time. A balanced stance gives you a solid, comfortable base to work from, helps reduce tension and fear, and makes possible most of the other Absolutes.

2. *Rhythm and movement in the stance.* Although it isn't always obvious, good hitters always have some kind of movement in the stance. They're like a car with its engine idling just before you pop the clutch. They can thus be quicker and shift their weight more effectively than someone who stands dead still.

3. *A good weight shift from a firm, rigid backside forward to hit from a firm, rigid frontside.* A hitter must shift his weight back in order to go forward. Balance and rhythm make this possible. Generally, the better the weight shift, the harder you hit the ball.

4. *Striding with the front toe closed.* Striding with your front toe pointing out at the pitcher pulls you out of position, causes your hip to open, and throws off the mechanics of your swing.

5. *Having the bat in the launching position at the moment the front foot touches down.* It's hard to see with the naked eye, but no matter where the bat is when they're in their stance, all good hitters have it in the launching position when their front foot completes the stride. They all step to swing. They never combine the two motions.

6. *Making a positive, aggressive motion back toward the pitcher.* That's where the ball's coming from and that's where you should try to hit it back. Good hitters go into the ball to hit it.

7. *A tension-free swing.* An enemy of his own creation, tension is one of a batter's biggest problems. It prevents full extension; it causes your head to move the wrong way; and it destroys the fluid, graceful swing that's ideal for hitting the ball.

8. *Putting your head down when you swing.* Good hitters see the ball longer and more often than poor hitters. And the reason good hitters do is that they lower their heads to watch the ball at the moment of contact. This is the most important Absolute of all, but it's impossible to do if you're not balanced or if you're tense.

9. *Using the whole field to hit in.* Only rarely will a good hitter limit himself by trying to pull the ball. Historically, as well as today, good hitters have hit to all fields. And in so doing, they have also gotten plenty of home runs without being crippled by tension and the other problems that afflict home-run-conscious hitters.

10. *Hit through the ball.* A good follow-through is essential to hitting the ball well. You can't afford to stop short or slack off at the last part of the swing. If you quit too soon, if you don't hit *through* the ball, none of the other Absolutes will do you much good.

APPLYING THE ABSOLUTES

If you watch much baseball, particularly on television, where the cameras give you different views than you get at the ball park, you may have noticed that batting stances and hitting styles are as individualized as fingerprints. And you may wonder when you see a good hitter with an especially unusual stance whether he's really demonstrating the techniques mentioned above.

He may not be. Without seeing the actual batter, it's impossible to tell. But I think it's likely that he is demonstrating the Absolutes or some variation of them but that the swing happens so fast that the untrained eye has difficulty picking them up.

If you had a videotape recorder and could slow the action down, you'd see what I mean. Whether the batter starts with the bat held vertically out in front of him, horizontally over his shoulder, cocked with his hands up by his face, or anyplace else, if he's a good hitter he will still have the bat in the launching position by the time his front foot hits. He will still shift his weight forward to the front leg, bring the bat forward so that it's out in front of him with full arm extension, and have his head down and eyes on the ball at the point of contact.

In other words, no matter where they start from or how they get there, all good hitters arrive at the same spots at critical moments. The same is true of a good hitter's rhythm. In some guys the movement back and forth is so obvious that anybody can see it. But in others it's so subtle that it's almost an internal weight shift and you have to be standing very close to the man to see it. But it's there all the same.

It's important to realize how these techniques apply. They may be Absolutes, but that doesn't mean they can't be personalized. In fact, they *have* to be personalized. Previous training, body type, talent, psychological outlook, and dozens of other factors make each player different. You can't take a rigid formula for hitting and make everyone conform exactly. The variations are rarely large. Usually it's a question of a few fractions of an inch one way or another, and a player can easily make such personalized adjustments without destroying the benefits the Absolutes provide.

Rhythm and movement aren't always easy to see in the stance itself. But one thing everyone sees are the practice swings many hitters take before settling into the stance. Often this is where the hitter's in-stance rhythm begins, since it gets him shifting his weight forward and back.

These photos show George Brett completing his last practice swing before going into his stance. As you look at them, pay particular attention to George's feet. Notice how the left foot comes up as he shifts his weight forward in photos 2-1 through 2-3. In photo 2-4, his weight is centered, but it moves back as his right foot rises in 2-5. The last photo shows him bringing his bat up and moving it into position as he assumes his stance.

A balanced, workable stance. George's weight is back. He's bent at the waist and his knees are slightly flexed. He's ready but also relaxed.

Here you can get some idea of why rhythm and movement in the stance are so important. Because of his rhythm George has no trouble shifting his weight back onto his rear leg (photos 2-9 through 2-11). His rear leg is stiff and rigid and his weight shift caused his front foot to come up off the ground. By photo 2-12 the backward weight shift is nearly complete and the forward weight shift starts as George begins his stride (photo 2-13).

Striding with the front toe closed leads to a powerful hitting position (photo 2-16). Notice the forward weight shift, the positive and aggressive motion back toward the pitcher, and the fact that the hips are still closed (that is, they haven't been turned outward toward the pitcher). Also notice that the bat is in the launching position at the moment the front foot hits the ground.

The weight shift forward to a firm, rigid front leg continues as George watches the incoming ball. Notice how a good weight shift causes the back toe to come up off the ground and how the hips don't open until George begins to bring the bat through (photos 2-18 through 2-19). In photo 2-21 George's head is down and his eyes are right on the ball. There's no doubt that he's going to hit it.

You may also see professional players who clearly don't demonstrate the Absolutes yet still manage to hit the ball. And you may also wonder why, if the Absolutes are so essential to hitting, more players don't try to apply them.

In answer to the first question, yes, it is possible for a player to hit without clearly demonstrating the techniques I've been talking about. But often he will have to compensate in some way for an Absolute he doesn't observe. And while he may hit occasionally or have a temporary hot streak, I don't think he can be consistent and still disregard the Absolutes.

As to why more batters don't incorporate these techniques in their swing, there are two answers. First, they may not be aware of the techniques. And second, they may not be willing to change. Professional baseball players tend to resist anything that may interfere with what they regard as a good swing. They don't want to fool around with a swing that's been good enough to help them win a major-league contract, even if making an adjustment here or there could produce better results. Then too, some of them are so pull-conscious that they don't want to hear about good, consistent hitting.

On the other hand, you've got players who are "comfortable" hitting around .230 or .240. They've got a good job and make a nice living without having to work too hard. They have no desire to improve, especially if it means working to break the ingrained but often bad habits they've gotten used to.

In either case, the player is less than receptive to a hitting coach's suggested improvements. However, when their batting averages begin to fall or when they're doing so poorly that they're in danger of being released, it's remarkable how attentive they can suddenly become.

2-20

2-21

The "Absolutes" of Good Hitting

It's a split second after contact, and George's head is down, his front leg is rigid, and he has good arm extension (photo 2-22-24). The swing has been powerful, but at the same time graceful and tension-free. Looking at photos 2-24, 2-25, and 2-26, you can see why a good baseball swing is often compared to a good golf swing—the smoothness and fluidity used to hit through the ball are very similar.

Also notice that not until 2-27 does George move his head. He didn't jerk his head up to see where the ball went. He put his head down and kept it there until long (relatively speaking) after the moment of contact.

Hitting through the ball is essential, and that means completing the swing with a good follow-through. As you can see here, the follow-through should be smooth and graceful, the natural result of everything that has come before it.

BAD HABITS MAKE BAD HITTERS

I don't think there's any question that a lot of the problems hitters of all ages experience are due to bad habits and well-meant but misguided instruction. If a player has been taught to roll his top hand over, for example, that motion becomes a part of his swing. He may have been doing it since he first began playing ball, and the habit gets reinforced every time he steps up to bat. Under such circumstances, it can be very difficult to get him to change, even when you both know it will make him a better ballplayer.

Recently, though, things have begun to change. At every level, from the grass roots on up, coaches and instructors are paying much more attention to the analysis and mechanics of the proper swing. As that process continues and as today's youngsters develop better habits and work their way up to the major leagues, you'll see more professional players demonstrating the Absolutes.

AIMING AT "PERFECT"

Finally, it's important to make clear that what I'm going to be describing in the following chapters is the "perfect" swing, one that incorporates all of the Absolutes and gives you the best chance to hit the ball. But in reality, even among the top professional hitters, the "perfect" swing is quite rare. In game situations even the best batter may take only one "perfect" swing in a hundred. There are just too many variables for it to be otherwise.

Yet as George Brett (1979: 645 AB/119 R/212 H/23 HR/107 RBI/.329) and other top hitters have repeatedly demonstrated, by striving

The "Absolutes" of Good Hitting

29

for the ideal you come a lot closer to perfection than most of your competitors. To me, that's what it's all about. I teach the ideal, knowing full well that it can rarely be completely achieved. But I also know that a player will come closer to perfection and hit the ball better and more often by striving for something that may be a little out of reach than if he makes some lesser target his goal.

HITTER ANALYSIS

JOHNNY BENCH
HEIGHT: 6 feet, 1 inch
WEIGHT: 197 pounds
AVERAGE (lifetime): .267

Here's Johnny Bench showing us that the head goes down when you swing and providing such a good example of complete arm extension that the shot almost looks posed. It wasn't, though. It was taken during the 1975 World Series.

A very strong player with a muscular swing, Bench has been known for being dominant with his top hand. He's tried to pull all his life and, I think, has been inconsistent because of it. His mechanics have not been the best, but he's been able to use his tremendous strength to compensate for many of his deficiencies. And, of course, he's been able to get full extension in spite of the way he rolls his top hand. In many seasons this has made him a dangerous hitter and a good RBI man.

Johnny Bench has also been a very durable catcher, and as a former catcher myself, I know this has an effect. For one thing, even with the newer gloves, your hands are always sore. Also, your legs take a beating, and you tire more quickly than any other player on the team except the pitcher. So you try to compensate somehow. I think Johnny Bench could be a better hitter if he weren't so pull-conscious, but I also think that when you consider injuries and everything else, he's been a superb player.

HITTER ANALYSIS

TED WILLIAMS
HEIGHT: 6 feet, 3 inches
WEIGHT: 205 pounds
AVERAGE (lifetime): .344

For 18 years, from 1939 through 1960 with time out for military service in the Second World War and the Korean conflict, Ted Williams dominated home plate in the American League. With more league batting championships (6) than any other player over the same time period, Williams averaged below .300 only once (.254 in 1959) and hit .406 in 1941. He also led the league in home runs four times, with 37 in '41, 36 in '42, 32 in '47, and 43 in '49.

A player of great God-given ability and profound dedication, you can see one of the reasons for his success in this picture. Williams here is in what might be called the "attack position." His bat is ready to be launched. He's doing a good job of shifting his weight. And most important of all, he's going to the ball to hit it.

I think one of the reasons Ted was able to attack so effectively has to do with his mental approach to the game. Ted always seemed to know *what* and *where* the ball was going to be and could thus prepare his attack accordingly. As a young kid I was catching when Williams was hitting, and I don't remember ever seeing him get fooled on a pitch.

I'm sure this was because he was very aware of pitchers and the patterns they tend to follow. In fact, while many other batters may have made a habit of asking themselves what the pitcher was going to throw next or how he'd respond to a particular situation, Ted Williams was the first to really bring this into focus. He was the first to talk about pitching patterns and the first to say, in effect, "Hey, look, there's more to hitting than just walking up to the plate with the bat. You don't have to leave it all to chance. There are ways to prepare yourself by figuring out what the pitcher's going to throw."

There's also something else Ted said in an interview once that I think ought to be mentioned. "Of course, everybody's trying to hit home runs, and, of course, everybody can't hit home runs and still be a good consistent hitter. It's too bad that more fellows don't realize this, because they're making themselves .230, .240, or .250 hitters when they could very well be .310, .320, or .340 hitters." I couldn't agree more.

HITTER ANALYSIS

TY COBB
HEIGHT: 6 feet, 1 inch
WEIGHT: 175 pounds
AVERAGE (lifetime): .367

At one time Ty Cobb held the record for the most bases stolen (96) in a single season. That mark, set in 1915, stood until 1962, when it was surpassed by Maury Wills with 104 stolen bases. (The current champ, of course, is Lou Brock, with 118 in 1974.) Now you may wonder what Cobb's stolen bases have to do with his hitting prowess. But in an odd way they are related because they both were influenced by what's come to be known as the "dead-ball era."

The baseballs in use during most of Cobb's career (1905–28) looked about the same as the ones we use today, but they didn't go as far when you hit them. Yet since that was all they had, that's what they played with. After the First World War, however, improved machinery and materials made it possible to produce baseballs with more zip in them. These were called "lively balls" and they soon put an end to the "dead-ball era."

The point is that during the time Cobb was playing, stealing a base wasn't such a bad idea. In fact, since the ball didn't go all that far, it could sometimes be even more advantageous to steal than to wait for the batter to hit it. The lively ball, however, went much farther when hit, making it generally more advantageous for base runners to wait until the batter connected before taking off.

The dead ball was also a major influence on the batter's whole approach to hitting. Since the ball didn't go as far, home runs were hit far less frequently. There was much more emphasis put on the base hit. Admittedly this is informed speculation on my part. I haven't really looked into it in depth. But based on conversations with old-time players, I think maybe guys in Cobb's era tried for the percentage. They aimed at hitting .300 and concentrated on making contact instead of pulling the ball.

Ty Cobb's record certainly seems to bear this out. He got more hits (4,191) than anyone else in the history of the sport. For nine consecutive years (1907–15) he held the American League batting title, and in two of those years he hit over .400 (.420 in 1911 and .410 in 1912). Tris Speaker aced him out in 1916. But he was again on top from 1917 through 1919. There just wasn't anyone else like him.

I never saw him, of course, but I think Ty Cobb could probably do anything he wanted to do with a baseball. And I think you can see some of the reasons why in this photo. The first thing you notice is the fact that he has gone back to go forward. He's clearly going to have an excellent weight shift. Second, his front leg is just about ready to stride, and his bat is already very close to the launching position. And third, he's choked up on the bat.

I don't like the fact that his hands are split. But leaving that aside, I think choking up probably gave him a lot of bat control. I've seen a lot of guys be successful doing it. When you see his powerful, basically sound mechanics and look at the amazing record, you can't help wondering what Ty Cobb would have done with the baseballs of today.

The "Absolutes" of
Good Hitting

35

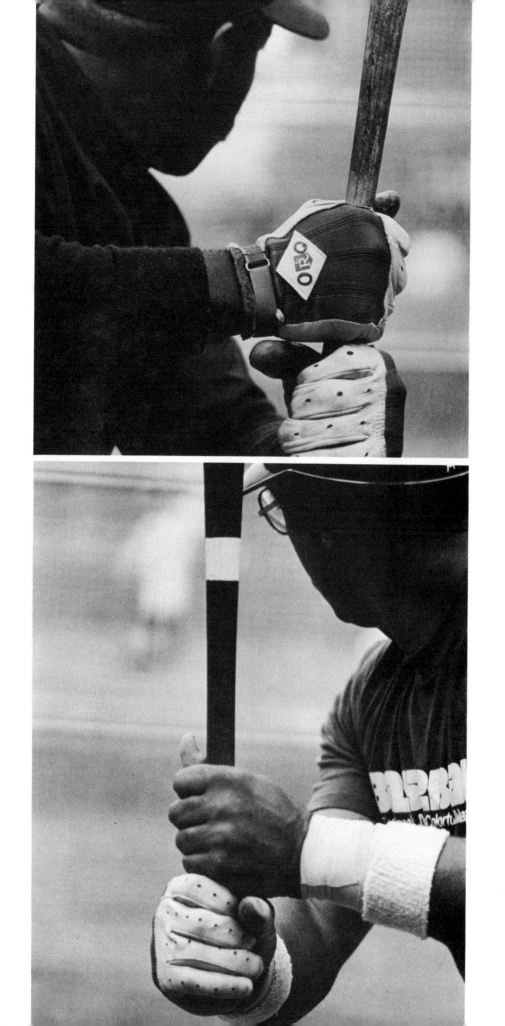

3
A NATURAL GRIP AND A BALANCED STANCE

There's nothing easy about hitting, but I think people often make it harder than it has to be. A good example of what I mean is the overemphasis on grip that seems to pervade baseball circles throughout the country. In the clinics that I give I try to present the whole picture of what it takes to be a better hitter. Yet time after time I run into a situation where all anyone wants to do is to argue and talk for half an hour or more about grip. It's almost as if people feel there's some kind of magic involved, as if the right grip will somehow transform them into great hitters.

Well, there isn't any magic. There's common sense. And common sense tells you that grip is important, that it has its place. But it's not the be-all and end-all of good hitting. As long as you've got a grip that is comfortable and that allows you a maximum amount of flexibility, you'll be fine.

TRY FOR A HAPPY MEDIUM

This is why I think the old rule about aligning your knuckles as you grip the bat is so wrong. Some players are still taught that they should line up

Your grip should be firm, of course. But it should also be relaxed and comfortable. I suggest forgetting about aligning your knuckles and simply grip the bat naturally.

3-1

either the knuckles closest to the hand or the knuckles forming the first joint of the fingers when holding the bat. But if you try this, you'll find that either way you end up with an awkward, uncomfortable grip that reduces your flexibility and cheats you out of a whole range of movement.

It's much better to try for something in the middle and forget about the two knuckle-aligning extremes. The same thing goes for where you place the bat in your hands (palms versus fingers) and how much pressure you apply. Holding the bat too deep in the palms reduces flexibility, while using your fingers too much makes your grip less secure. Again, try for the happy medium, with the bat held so that it crosses the area where your palm ends and your fingers begin, the place where you usually get calluses if you do much work with your hands.

It's especially important to hold your bat this way with your top hand if it is more dominant than your bottom one. If that's the case, you could use more of your palm in your bottom-hand grip. But these are refinements. Holding the bat across the callus area of both hands is a good place to start. Later you can make fine adjustments for comfort and control.

3-2

Each individual is different, and there are thus many effective ways to grip a bat. However, regardless of how big or how strong your hands are, be careful not to get the bat so far back into the palm that your flexibility is reduced. Laying the bat across the place where your fingers join your palm is a good, happy medium.

3-3

It's a fine point, but if you have an especially dominant top hand, you might want to hold the bat more in the fingers like this.

3-4

White knuckles. Compare this photo with the easy, natural grip shown in photo 3-1. Notice how the thumb is clamped down and how the fingers and hands show the tension.

The tension of the white-knuckle syndrome, doesn't stay in the hands. It works its way up your arms and into your body until you're tense all over.

WATCH OUT FOR WHITE KNUCKLES

It's rare that you'll find a player who doesn't hold his bat firmly enough. The real headache is the other extreme, what I call the "white-knuckle syndrome." Some players grip the bat so tightly that you almost want to look to see if they've left finger depressions in the wood. There are lots of reasons for this (force of habit, fear, an overwhelming desire to get a hit, and so forth), but the result is always the same: tension.

Tension is one of the biggest enemies a hitter has. Yet by gripping the bat so hard that his knuckles turn white, a player *guarantees* that he will become tense. The tension doesn't stay just in the hands. It always works its way up, cording the muscles in the arms, tightening up the shoulders, stiffening the neck, until the player is tense all over.

Don't grip the bat like your life depended upon it. Ease up. Your body knows how firmly you have to hold the bat to do the job. So let it take over. I'd even go so far as to say, "Don't think about the problem unless you've got to counteract tension." Or, in other words, just pick up the bat and grip it naturally.

BATS, RAGS, AND GLOVES

Now, about the size bat you use and where you should hold it. I used to believe in having the player choke up on the bat to make it more manageable. And I still think it's a good idea. But over the years I've found that players just won't do it. So instead, I suggest going to a shorter bat.

But here you run into problems—ego problems and *macho* self-image problems. Psychologists could argue for days over why many players feel they've got to swing a big club. All I know is that there are an awful lot of players at all levels of the game using bats that are too big for them. Not that you can't use a big bat to get a hit. Many of them can and do. But they'd get even *more* hits with slightly shorter, more maneuverable bats.

Dave Duncan, the player I was asked to coach at Oakland, is a good example. Here was a big, strong, talented boy who had a big, loopy swing. One season Dave hit fifty or more home runs playing minor league ball, but he couldn't hit in the big leagues. The two of us made some adjustments in his swing that worked pretty well. But we also agreed to change where he gripped the bat.

Dave would go up to the plate trying to hit home runs and holding the bat near the knob, as he always did. But as soon as he had two strikes on him, we had him choke up an inch or so on the bat and try to hit the ball back through the middle. I kept track. Dave hit sixteen homers that year—twelve of which were hit when he had two strikes and had choked up on the bat.

So if you're in a situation where you don't have much of a selection, don't be afraid to pick a bat and choke up on it to make it more manageable. And when you go to buy a bat, don't let yourself get suckered into buying one that gives you more length than you need.

What's the right length for you? I can't say. There's no rule of thumb I know of that will produce good results. I suggest that you experiment with a lot of different lengths, barrel sizes, and so forth until you find a combination you like.

Nor can I advise you on other features you'll find in a bat. In the Yankee clubhouse we've got a closet the size of a small bedroom that's filled with bats of every description. There are bats with a dished-out area in the tip, bats with three-inch knobs, bats with no knob at all, and every size knob in between. You can also find bats with depressions in the handle molded to fit the fingers, bats with cork grips, and bats stained a variety of dark colors.

In the end it's all a matter of what works best for you. The only thing I'd caution you about is that, just as with the grip, there's no magic to the kind of bat you choose. A bat can never take the place of practice, dedication, and hard work.

Whether you use a pine-tar rag and/or a batting glove or gloves is also a matter of personal preference. When I was playing I couldn't hit unless I had my bat taped up in a certain way and unless I wiped the handle with the pine-tar rag before stepping into the box. This combination gave me just the right feel on the bat. Some players make the bat so sticky with pine tar that it's a wonder they don't end up carrying it to first base with them when they get a hit. Other players don't use any at all. Lou Piniella, in fact, rubs dirt on his hands and bat before going to the plate to make it more slippery. But it works for him, just as pine tar works for others. And that's what's important.

Batting gloves are relatively new additions to the game. Young kids wear them, I think, because they see the big leaguers wearing them. And the professionals got started because when you're hitting continuously in batting practice a glove can really save your hand from stinging.

The old-timer image of a ballplayer as a hard-swinging, tobacco-spitting, rough, tough, s.o.b. who laughed at pain and disdained physical comfort is fading fast. I remember, for example, when as a converted infielder, I started catching. They handed me one of the fat, no-break catcher's gloves used at the time and told me I had to catch two-handed. Yet every guy I ever saw who was trying to teach me that technique had fingers so gnarled and bent that they could barely move. I took one look at their hands and decided I wasn't so all-fired sure two-handed catching made any sense.

Eventually some free-thinking souls allowed catchers to use one-handed gloves. And damned if they didn't work out better than the old doughnut-shaped ones. I think the same thing holds true for batting gloves. Today a lot of catchers and infielders wear batting gloves or golf gloves under their mitts to reduce the sting of the ball. A lot of batters wear them on one or both hands for the same reason, and I don't see anything wrong with it.

BALANCE! BALANCE! BALANCE!

Balance is a crucial factor in any sport. Golf, tennis, football, basketball—take your pick. You'll never see a successful performer in any of these activities who isn't on balance most of the time. The same thing is true in baseball. Balance is so vital to successful hitting that I can only believe that people who don't emphasize it don't recognize its true importance.

Balance is the foundation that makes so many of the other Absolutes possible. It lessens the fear that all batters have and lets them make that positive and aggressive motion back at the pitcher. It makes them less reluctant to put their heads down to watch the ball. It makes it easier to develop a rhythm and a good weight shift, to stride properly, and to do almost everything else you must do to hit the ball.

Small wonder that balance is one of the chief goals of a batter's stance. A workable stance is one that enables you to be balanced completely through the swing, and it starts, logically enough, with the feet.

If I were to coach a hundred kids who'd never played baseball before, I'd have them all begin by placing their feet a shoulder's width apart. You've got to have a place to start from, and the way the human body's designed, this makes the most sense. After about two weeks of practice, I'd wager that about ninety of the players would be doing well with their feet in that position. Ten would probably need a little adjustment one way or the other.

The key thing is to find a position that allows you to be completely balanced and to shift your weight easily back toward the catcher and forward toward the pitcher as you swing. You probably won't have to make much of an adjustment from the shoulder's-width starting point. But if you do, guard against making your stance too wide. The problem of too narrow a stance, like that of too loose a grip, doesn't come up very often. But many batters have a definite tendency to let their front foot creep forward. Their feet get farther and farther apart until they have real difficulty shifting their weight during the swing or striding forward with their front foot at the proper moment.

OPEN, CLOSED, OR SQUARE?

There are three types of stances in baseball: the open, the closed, and the square or parallel. Each has its defenders and detractors. In the open stance the front foot is pointed out toward the field at somewhere around a forty-five-degree angle to the head-to-toe center line of your body. This, some people argue, makes it easier to pull the ball. And generally that's true, since with your front foot in that position, you're set up to reach out and hit the ball in front of the plate.

In the closed stance your front foot points more or less straight ahead, but it is somewhat forward of a line drawn through the toes of your back foot. Proponents of the closed stance say that it puts the batter in position to hit the ball to the opposite field, as when a right-hander hits it to right field or a left-hander hits it to left field. And that's true too, since having your front foot slightly forward makes it easier for you to reach forward to get that kind of ball.

3-10

3-12

3-13

A stance like this, with feet about a shoulder's width apart, is an excellent place to start (photo 3-10).

Batters who let their front foot creep forward over time eventually end up with a stance similar to this, or worse. As you can see, shifting your weight in a stance like this is much more difficult than the one shown in photo 3-10.

The open stance.

The closed stance.   *The square or parallel stance.*

The trouble is that while each of these stances makes it easier to hit one kind of pitch, it simultaneously increases the difficulty of hitting the other. It's very tough, for example, to pull a ball from a closed stance. Most who try it end up rushing their swing, muscling the ball, and rolling their wrists over. I'm not saying it's impossible to both hit the other way (to the opposite field) and pull the ball from an open or a closed stance, but it takes an individual with special talent and with complete mental and physical control.

This is one reason why I favor the square or parallel stance. With your feet parallel, you're not precommitted and are free to do just about anything you want. You can pull; you can hit to the opposite field; you can hit the fast ball, the curve ball, and anything else the pitcher cares to throw. In addition, when you're in a parallel stance, your balance is better. The open and the closed stances tend to be awkward because they make it difficult to get your weight onto the balls of your feet, where it must be if you are to be balanced.

**A Natural Grip and
a Balanced Stance**

45

It's also important to have a comfortable, level place to stand in the box, which is why you see players pawing the dirt with their spikes before settling into their stance. With eighteen guys using the batter's box repeatedly during a game, holes and bumps in the dirt inevitably develop. Some players probably make too big a deal out of digging at the ground and tapping the dirt off their spikes with the bat. But a comfortable, level place to stand is so important to good balance that I can't criticize them for it.

THE "READY" POSITION

When you've got your feet into position, the next step is to get your body into position too. That means bending forward at the waist and softening

As George Brett is demonstrating here, when you bend forward at the waist your weight comes forward onto your toes.

When you bend at the waist first . . .

your knees in much the same way you do in tennis when you're waiting for your opponent to return the ball. This is your "ready" position. Bending forward brings your body's center of gravity closer to the ground, and that, combined with a softening or slight bending of the knees, makes it possible for you to *move* when the time comes.

The key thing to remember about assuming the ready position is to avoid getting into it all at once. Make it a deliberate, two-step operation by bending at the waist *first* and softening the knees *second*. In addition, if you bend your knees first instead of waiting, your weight won't come forward when you bend at the waist. Although you may think you're balanced, your weight will really be back on your heels instead of on your toes, where it should be. Make a habit of bending first at the waist, then at the knees, and you'll always achieve the correct position.

. . . and then soften your knees, you virtually guarantee yourself good balance when you assume your final stance.

If you don't bend first at the waist and then at the knees, this may be the result. You may think you're balanced, but your weight is really back on your heels instead of forward on your toes.

Depending upon the player, any of these starting bat positions or some position in between will work. There's the nearly vertical (3-20), the nearly vertical held out in front, the middle position (3-22 and 3-23), and the flat position, in which the bat actually touches the shoulder (3-24). The important thing is to start as close to the launching position as you comfortably can.

The launching position. Taken just after the front foot hits the ground, this picture shows where the bat must go, regardless of where it starts in the stance. Compare this with photos 3-20 through 3-24.

At this point some people advocate deliberately cocking or coiling the upper body by twisting back away from the pitcher's mound. The amount of coil is determined by the individual and by what it takes for him to put maximum force behind the ball. Yet, while it's true that you must coil a little to hit the ball well, I've found that emphasizing this fact leads to all kinds of problems. Things work out much better if you concentrate instead on where you hold the bat and how far back you keep your hands. If you do that, the cocking or coiling of the upper body tends to take care of itself.

THE LAUNCHING POSITION

In 1973 I photographed the All-Star Game with a high-speed (sixty frames per second) camera. In analyzing the films after the game, I found that regardless of his personal style or where he started his swing, every hitter in both leagues had the bat in the same position when his front foot touched down to complete the stride. I had analyzed a lot of film and tape before and have analyzed a lot since, and in every case the results are the same. All good, consistent hitters bring their bat to that same spot at the same time. I call this spot the "launching position," and it's clearly one of the Absolutes.

In the launching position, your hands are back. The bottom hand is at about the same level as the letters on your uniform—that is, on a line drawn across your upper chest. The top hand is just off the rear tip of your shoulder. The bat is held above the back of your shoulder at about a forty-five-degree angle to the ground. The bat isn't flat and it isn't straight up and down.

Now, knowing that the bat has to get there to swing, doesn't it make sense to *start* as close to the launching position as possible when you take your stance? You bet it does. There has to be some movement, of course, to overcome inertia and give the bat momentum. But the less distance the bat has to travel to get to the launching position, the less chance there is of making a mistake along the way. This makes you quicker, gives you

This is an example of the wrapped position used by many pull hitters. To get to the launching position from here, a batter has to bring the bat down and then up again for a big, loopy swing. Compare this with the more workable positions shown.

more time to react, and not coincidentally, makes you a more consistent hitter.

The importance of starting near the launching position can best be seen in a negative example: the pull hitter. Pull hitters usually have big, floppy swings. A lot of them start in a "wrapped" position with their hands up near the head, and the bat twisted so far back and around that the bat head points toward the pitcher. To get to the launching position, they must take a hitch down (bring the bat down) and then roll their wrists to take a hitch up and over a hump. It's hard to see with the naked eye. But when you slow the motion down photographically, you see that the bat arcs through a loop to get to the launching position.

A big, loopy swing is the problem that keeps an awful lot of young boys from becoming major-league hitters, and a lot of major leaguers from becoming really good hitters. For one thing, the extra distance the bat must travel means the player with a big swing must react faster than someone starting closer to the launching position. That's bad enough when the big-swinging player is trying for a simple base hit. But when he tries to pull the ball, it's even worse. Since pulling the ball requires a player to hit it out in front of the plate, he's got to react even *faster*. Rushing a swing like that creates tension and reduces control. This is why pull hitters are usually inconsistent.

Players with a big swing have a big hole, a large area where they *cannot* hit the ball. Pitchers know this, of course, and most do their best to put the ball exactly in that spot, which is why pull hitters strike out so often. The pitch that does them in is usually either one that's high and inside or one that's low and away.

Now, "high and tight" or "low and away" is how you're supposed to pitch everybody. But these pitches are especially damaging to the pull hitter. If a pull hitter swings at anything above the belt (high) he's almost sure to miss it. And for a very simple reason. That's right where the arc in their swing is. Pull hitters tend to swing up. So any ball that's high or "up and in" is almost physically impossible for them to hit. They can't put the bat on a ball that's in the loop of their swing.

About the only pitch a pull hitter can hit well is the one low (between the belt and the knees) and in. But if the ball is low and also curving away from him, he'll have problems. As he reaches out to hit it (as he must if he's trying to pull), he has to roll his wrists over and toward the pitcher's mound to get the bat on the ball. That's almost impossible to do. But even if he succeeds, his hands and arms are in an extremely weak position, too weak to hit the ball very far, let alone pull a home run.

Consequently, when the scouts sign big, muscular pull hitters and ask me to teach them how to make contact, I usually begin by shortening their swings. Having them start with their bats closer to the launching position reduces the distance the bat head must travel by anywhere from 20 to 30 percent. And it's fascinating to watch the result.

All of a sudden the players find they don't have to react as quickly. In fact, the first thirty pitches they swing at are usually hit foul because they're accustomed to having to react so fast that they don't correct for the extra time they now have. They are amazed at how quick they are. If the player is willing, the adjustments in timing can be made easily enough, with improved control, reduced tension, and greater consistency as results.

Some players, though, aren't willing to shorten their swings because they're afraid of losing power. Granted, with a big, long arc of a swing, if you do hit the ball you hit it a little harder. But you don't hit it as often. By shortening up the swing, a player may sacrifice a little power (not much, but a little). Yet when a strong player connects with a short, compact swing, the ball still goes a long way.

Because a shorter swing makes you quicker, it gives you more time to look at the ball. And the longer you can watch the ball, the less chance there is that you will be fooled by a breaking ball or any other kind of pitch. You'll also find that your new quickness makes it easier to hit the ball out in front of the plate when you have to pull.

WHAT TO AVOID

As you can see, there are a lot of reasons for holding your bat as close to the launching position as you can when you take your stance. However, the bat position in the stance should also be comfortable and tension-free. So in some cases modifications may have to be made. This is best done by experimenting, with the aid of your coach if possible.

But there are certain pitfalls to avoid. Be careful not to bring your hands too far back, since that will lengthen your swing and create muscular tension. It can also cause you to "bring your hands with you" as your upper body turns toward the pitcher. This makes it difficult to extend your arms and swing the way you should. Players with "slow bats" are usually players who start with their hands too far back.

You should also avoid holding the bat vertically. A forty-five-degree angle is the ideal, but a bat that is held flatter or more parallel to the ground will still work. The same isn't true, though, of increasing the angle in the opposite direction, approaching a straight up-and-down position.

Now I know what you're thinking: What about the vertical bat associated with Boston's Carl Yastrzemski? And you've got a point. A vertical bat has worked well for him. But only because of his superb mastery of mind and body. Few professionals and even fewer amateurs have that kind of control. Yaz is just a very special case.

You may also have seen some professional players take a hitch down to bring their bat into position. This will work, but unless your body type or batting style makes it absolutely necessary, I strongly suggest that you avoid it.

Finally, once you've found the bat position that's right for you,

Look what happens when you stand too close to the plate. A good, level swing puts your hands right in the strike zone while the meat of the bat ends up over the opposite batter's box.

practice achieving it whenever you step up to the plate. This will be much easier if you establish a reference point first. If you just put your bat into position without touching it to your body, you can never really be sure of where it is. That's why a lot of players will touch the bat to their shoulder or their ear and *then* raise it to the correct position. This contact or reference point lets them start from the same place each time, and many good hitters make the procedure part of their batting routine.

DISTANCE TO THE PLATE AND PLATE COVERAGE

Many players at all levels have a bad habit of constantly creeping up on the plate. Over a period of time they gradually move closer and closer, until they're eventually standing so close that they all but destroy their chances of hitting. This is ironic because an intense desire to hit the ball and hit it really hard is usually the reason they get so close. It doesn't make sense, but that's what happens.

A Natural Grip and a Balanced Stance

Ideally, you should stand in a spot that will allow you to fully extend your arms when you swing. You should be able to put the meat of the bat on the ball, have plenty of time to react to a pitch, and be able to take that positive, aggressive stride toward the ball as you swing. Standing too close defeats all of these goals and creates several other problems besides.

To hit well, you've got to be bent at the waist, your head has to go down as you watch the ball, and you've got to make contact with the meat of the bat. If you attempt to do these things when you're too close to the plate, you end up stepping away from where you want to hit the ball and bending your body back and away as you struggle to put the bat on the ball. If you try to pull, you find you have to straighten up even more. This makes it impossible to stride positively toward the ball and often results in a batter throwing his upper body back and shying away at the point of contact. That's no way to hit a baseball.

But it gets worse. The closer you are to the plate, the quicker you have to react. At some point a batter may do well standing close. He may even hit a home run or two. But eventually he creeps so close that he misses the ball he could have hit for a homer if he'd been farther away. Because of the quicker reaction time required, batters who crowd the plate are also especially vulnerable to an off-speed pitch like a change-up or a breaking ball.

"But what about plate coverage?" people ask. Well, though it may be surprising, I don't think plate coverage per se is all that important. And I don't think there's a really good rule of thumb most players can use. I've

When you back off the plate and take a more moderate position like this . . .

. . . you get just the kind of plate coverage you need.

seen young hitters, for example, put the bat head on the outside part of the plate and use that as a way of determining how close to stand. But it doesn't really work.

Far more important, I think, is to look at your body type and then apply a little common sense. A guy with short arms who has trouble getting extended, for instance, will naturally have to stand closer to the plate than a tall man with good extension.

In addition, it's important to remember that when you're bent at the waist, your arm extension is different from when you're standing upright. If you bend or lean over a lot, for example, you can take your stance farther from the plate than someone who barely bends at all. Actually, getting a player to bend at the waist so that he's in a good ready position may be more important than worrying about his plate coverage.

HOW DEEP IN THE BOX?

Standing too deep in the box (too far back toward the catcher) or standing too far forward can cause several problems. The only positive aspect of standing deep in the box is that you can see the ball longer. This can be helpful when you're facing a pitcher who specializes in smoke and throws a really hard fast ball. But for my money it's outweighed by a couple of big negatives. When a player standing deep in the box sees the ball coming in he often feels he has to react and ends up swinging too soon. If, on the other hand, the batter reacts at the proper time, he may have trouble keeping the ball in fair territory without drastically shortening the follow-through of his swing.

Moving forward in the box lets you hit the ball sooner and thus makes it easier to take a full swing and still keep the ball inside the foul lines. Depending upon the player, there may even be a direct mathematical relation between the fractions of an inch he moves forward or back in the box and the number of feet fair or foul the ball goes. Hitting the ball sooner can be an advantage when you're facing a pitcher known for throwing sinkers, screwballs, or breaking balls because you catch them before they complete their break or drop. So at those times you might want to inch forward a little.

In general, though, you'll do best if you avoid extremes. Instead of standing too deep or too far forward, try for a middle position. The happy medium again. Usually, if you stand so that your front foot touches down near the middle of home plate when you take your stride, you'll be at a pretty good depth.

TAKE YOUR TIME SETTING UP

It ought to be clear by now that you can't just grab a bat and walk up to the plate if you want to be a successful hitter. Your stance is critical to your balance and weight shift, to your timing, to the quickness of your swing, to your lack of tension, and to just about every other aspect of hitting. Remember: A balanced, workable stance is an Absolute that makes nearly all of the other Absolutes possible. It's your foundation, so take your time and set it up right.

Good hitters spend a lot of time developing a workable stance and they're careful to maintain it each time they come up to bat. This is one reason why successful hitters will usually go through some little routine when they step up to the plate. Taking practice swings, bending at the waist and then softening the knees, touching the bat to the rear shoulder before raising it to a spot near the launching position, and so forth all help a player make certain he's in the proper stance. It's just too vital a factor to treat lightly.

HITTER ANALYSIS

LOU GEHRIG
HEIGHT: 6 feet
WEIGHT: 200 pounds
AVERAGE (lifetime): .340

Certainly one of the most talented men to ever play the game, the overwhelming impression that Lou Gehrig leaves on your mind is one of great strength. And it would take a strong man to hit four homers in one game, as he did in 1932, and to hit more home runs than anybody else in 1934 and 1936 (49 each time). Yet he was one of those rare players whose home-run hitting didn't stop him from compiling an impressive career batting average: .340, after 17 years during which he played in more consecutive games (2,130) than anyone else before or since.

Here you see Gehrig in 1935 posing for an Associated Press photographer. Yet although the shot is posed and although Gehrig is clearly more tense than he would be in action, he's still showing us two important things.

First, look at his bat position. Like Babe Ruth's, his bat is neither straight up and down nor parallel to the ground. It's in the middle and consequently will make for a smoother, more compact swing than either of the two extremes, something that can be very important to a man of Gehrig's strength and size. Also, the bat is held much closer to the launching position than with many of today's players, allowing him to wait a bit longer and to pick his pitches more effectively.

Now look at the grip. As you can see, it's quite natural. You don't see an artificial alignment of any two sets of knuckles. Even though he's a little tenser than he ordinarily would be, his grip still looks comfortable, as if he'd just picked up the bat and walked up to the plate prepared to hit. These two factors, of course, weren't the only things he had going for him, but I don't think there can be any doubt that they contributed to his success.

HITTER ANALYSIS

BABE RUTH

HEIGHT: 6 feet, 2 inches
WEIGHT: 215 pounds
AVERAGE (lifetime): .342

I never saw Ruth play, but I've seen a lot of pictures and film of him. And, although this shot of Ruth in his stance is posed, it's typical of the way he looked in actual play.

Several things stand out in this photo. First, the Babe used a parallel or square stance, with both feet pointing straight ahead. His eyes and his head are in exactly the right position. His head is turned far enough toward the pitcher to be able to see the ball with both eyes, but not so far that his upper body is forced out of line. Most important, his bat is neither vertical nor parallel to the ground. It's about midway between those two extremes, just where it ought to be to insure a smooth, hitch-free swing.

This is the bat position that makes the most sense from a mechanical standpoint. Yet although I knew this and had proved it often, it was still reassuring to go to an Old-Timers' Game at Yankee Stadium to see it demonstrated by great players from decades past.

These men were and are living records of the batting styles used years ago, and it was fascinating to watch them. None of them moved as fast as they did in their prime and some fairly tottered up to the plate. But all of them showed the world that they could still handle a bat, and damn near every one of them held his bat the way Ruth is holding his in this picture.

An Old Timers' Game in the future, featuring players who are active today, would tell a different story, for batting styles, like men's suit styles, seem to follow certain trends. The trends are most evident in the bat and body position, since that's when a player's stationary and most easily seen. I'm not sure I could prove it, but I think these trends are most influenced by the players who are most successful at the time.

Forty or fifty years ago, players held their bats more like Ruth—pointing somewhere between vertical and horizontal and held relatively close to the launching position. In the past twenty-five years or so, however, bats have become more vertical and are held higher or farther back. Yet, just because it's popular and a lot of players do it doesn't make it right. For reasons explained elsewhere, the players who imitated Babe Ruth's bat position forty years ago were much better off than those who follow the fashion of today.

If the greatest player the game has ever produced held his bat a certain way, you've just got to figure there's a reason. And there is. Whether Babe Ruth would have put it this way or not, the fact is that his bat position was based on the soundest possible mechanics.

**A Natural Grip and
a Balanced Stance**

59

HITTER ANALYSIS

MIKE SCHMIDT
HEIGHT: 6 feet, 2 inches
WEIGHT: 203 pounds
AVERAGE (1985): .277

With a total of 458 career home runs, Mike Schmidt has proved himself to be one of the premier sluggers of his generation. Mike had a horrendous start in 1985 but he made a remarkable recovery, hitting well over his .266 career average, while swatting 33 home runs. This made it eleven times in the last 12 years that Mike's hit over 30 homers in a season.

This photograph shows Mike fully extended with his head down as he strokes the ball for a base hit against the Cubs.

Mike is a fine example of starting with the front toe closed and having the bat in the launching position at the very moment the front foot touches the ground. In fact, beginning with his balanced, workable stance, Mike embodies just about every one of the Absolutes. He is in constant motion at the plate, wiggling, shaking his backside, for good rhythm and balance. He makes a positive, aggressive motion back toward the pitcher; he puts his head down when he swings; at the moment of contact his top hand is always underneath; he lands with his front toe closed with his weight shifted to the front. Even though he is probably better known as a pull hitter, he still has tremendous power to all fields.

Charley always felt that Mike would be a better, more effective hitter if he was off the plate a bit, which would give him better extension. About two or three years ago, Mike did move away from the plate, which allowed him to hit around the field a bit. Nevertheless, Mike manages to hit the ball a long way sometimes, even when he doesn't get his arms fully extended at impact.

HITTER ANALYSIS

STAN MUSIAL
HEIGHT: 6 feet
WEIGHT: 175 pounds
AVERAGE (lifetime): .331

As students of the game will remember, Stan Musial was known for his "unusual" stance. Yet he got more hits (3,630) than any other players but Ty Cobb and Henry Aaron, hit 475 home runs, and compiled a career average of .331. How could a player have such an unorthodox approach and still be so successful?

The answer is that in spite of appearances, Musial's stance and batting style were still mechanically sound and still firmly rooted in the Absolutes. He is perhaps the most dramatic example of what I've been saying all along. And that is that the Absolutes represent "perfection," something to strive for even though you know you may never achieve it and may have to adapt the various principles to suit certain other requirements along the way. Yet by having a goal to aim at, even if you fall short, you'll still come much closer and have more success than if you let everything happen by chance.

The exaggerated crouch Musial shows us in this picture is a case in point. There's no question but that he's bent farther forward than the ideal, and I doubt that many coaches would encourage their players to hit this way. Yet it may be that Musial's body type allowed him to feel most comfortable in this position. The important thing is that Musial was always *well balanced,* and that particular Absolute made this exaggerated crouch workable for him.

Or take his bat position. Musial held his bat nearly vertical and farther back toward the catcher than most other players. To many people it would look a little awkward. Yet he never seemed to have any trouble getting the bat to the launching position when his front foot hit as he took his stride. And as an Absolute, *that* was the truly important point.

Stan Musial was also a tension-free hitter—largely, I think, because he didn't try to pull the ball. Like nearly all great hitters, he used the whole field to hit in. In spite of his pose here, he used a closed stance and normally was back in the box. In fact, I think that in addition to his great ability, standing off the plate and going into the ball were probably the two most important factors in his success. They let him hit the ball where it was pitched and allowed him to develop the tremendous weight shift needed to hit the ball hard.

When you analyze it, you realize that Musial's stance and style weren't unorthodox at all. Granted they may have been unusual and somewhat exaggerated. But they were firmly grounded in good mechanics and ultimately represented his personal way of applying the Absolutes.

**A Natural Grip and
a Balanced Stance**

63

4
RHYTHM, WEIGHT SHIFT, AND STRIDE

I once worked with a batter who, although he was a pretty good ballplayer, was a notoriously weak breaking-ball hitter. He didn't have what you'd call an analytical approach to the problem, so sometimes it was difficult getting through to him. But one day he surprised me. We'd been working on his stride, trying to improve his weight shift. He had done pretty well and toward the end of batting practice he had really connected on a couple of my pitches.

I was walking off the mound, and he came running up to. me all excited. "Charley," he said, "I think I've got it. If I get to the right spot at the right time, I don't *care* whether it's a fast ball, a breaking ball, or anything else—I'll send it a mile!" I nodded and said, "Yep. You got it, all right."

To hear this player talk, you'd think he'd just discovered something brand new about baseball. And in a way he had, for what he discovered was certainly new to him. But actually, every experienced hitter has the same thought. He *knows* when he can hit and when he can't, when he's not getting to the right spot at the right time. But what a lot of hitters don't know is what to do to solve the problem. They leave it to chance and go to bat four or five times just praying to get a hit, to get back in the groove.

Most of the time their problems can be traced to their stride, the step a batter takes toward the pitcher to initiate the process of swinging. The hitters' stride is too long or too short, or it's mistimed or poorly coordinated with the rest of their body. They may be having trouble shifting their weight back and then forward, or they may lack the necessary rhythm to get things started properly.

You'd think a lot of these difficulties could be cleared up fairly easily by simply pointing out the problem and showing the player what he ought to be doing. But sadly enough, that isn't the case. This whole area of stride, weight shift, and rhythm is so misunderstood and so full of bad information that even some of the best players don't fully grasp its importance. Yet these points are so critical to effectively putting your body's maximum force behind the ball that they're Absolutes of good hitting. As a coach you sometimes want to bang your head against a wall when a player either can't or won't understand it.

It's particularly frustrating because the whole idea of rhythm and weight shift is so simple. If you've ever pounded a stake into the ground with a sledgehammer, taken an ax to a log or tree trunk, or cut a piece of wood with a handsaw, you've used exactly the same principles. Think of the rhythm you develop when you use a handsaw and the way you shift your weight forward and back, forward and back.

Or think of the way you bring a sledgehammer or ax over your head, down to the target, pause a second, and then bring the tool arcing back up, over, and down again. The rhythm and the alternating shifting of weight let you put your whole body into the task, maximizing the effect of each blow.

Which is *exactly* the same thing you want to do when you hit a baseball. The problem is that, unlike swinging an ax or driving a stake, hitting a baseball is not a continuous, ongoing process. It is, or at least it appears to be, a single, explosive swing taken from an all but stationary position. Consequently most people don't make the connection between swinging a bat and, say, swinging an ax or doing dozens of similar things that involve rhythm and weight shift. I know any number of players, for example, who bat from a dead stand, with no movement whatsoever until they take their stride. And I know a lot more who have never been able to understand that your weight has to go *back* toward the catcher before you can effectively shift it *forward* to meet the ball.

THE IMPORTANCE OF "BACK"

Baseball has a language all its own, and a term you might hear rather frequently if you spent much time around some batting cages is "back." Used as an adjective or as a noun, this is merely a short way of referring to having most of your weight on your rear leg before shifting it forward just after the stride.

I don't want to belabor the point, but I don't want there to be any misunderstanding either: You can't go forward if you don't go back first. You can prove this to yourself very easily. Stand upright with your feet a shoulder's width apart and try shifting your weight to the left so that most of it is on your left leg. Now try the same thing, only this time shift your weight over to your right leg first and *then* shift to the left. You'll see the difference immediately. By shifting to your right leg first, you get a much more effective transfer of weight onto your left leg.

That's what back is all about. It's simple. But what a difference it makes when you connect with the ball. Good hitters know this. And some, like Lou Piniella, often use it as a key mental image to help them hit. Often when Lou has a problem hitting, he'll say, "I'm not back." He knows that if he gets back he can go forward and hit the ball hard. But if he gets "against" he can't get his body transferring through the ball and consequently doesn't have enough power.

When Lou says "against," he means he has his weight against his back leg instead of on top of it. Which brings up a topic that has been a little controversial in professional baseball circles, namely, "How *far* back should your weight be?" Like so many other things, it's often a matter of degree, complicated by the fact that the same terms mean different things to different people.

If you stand with your feet a shoulder's width apart, your weight is what I would call "against" both legs, almost as if your upper body were resting on the peak of a triangle formed by both legs and an imaginary line between your two feet. If you shift so that one leg becomes completely vertical and maybe the opposite foot comes up off the floor, your weight is "on top" of the vertical leg.

Now, it may well be that the best weight shift back when you hit puts you someplace between "on top" and "against" your rear leg. I can't say for certain. But I do know you can't teach it that way. That's why I tell my players to get their weight back "on top" of the rear leg. As a mental image and a goal for the player to aim at, this seems to work best. I know full well that the player may not get completely on top, but by going in that direction he gets closer to where he ought to be.

If you're balanced and you're back, you should be able to take batting practice on one leg. And some players have even approached doing that in regular games. If you've ever seen pictures of Japan's leading hitter, Sadaharu Oh, you know that he lifts his front knee and brings his thigh up when he strides. Vic Davalillo used to do something similar, and Mel Ott used to kick his leg out a little. Unusual as they are, I think these moves are all mechanically sound. They all have the effect of getting the weight back on top of that rear leg before shifting it forward.

This is what's meant by "back." Notice that George clearly has most of his weight on his back leg. The front leg bears almost no weight and is ready to be picked up to begin the stride and weight shift. If you look closely, you'll also notice that the shoulder, hip, and back heel are all on the same vertical line. This is something I watch for as a coach, since the shoulder, hip, and heel should be aligned like this at some point in every swing if the batter is to have a good weight shift.

Compare this photo with photo 4-1. Here most of the weight is on the front leg or somewhere between the front and back legs. This doesn't give you much leeway for a good, positive weight shift. You could start from this position, though I think photo 4-1 is more workable. But if you don't go back from here, you'll have a lot of trouble shifting your weight for maximum effect.

RHYTHM AND MOVEMENT—AN ABSOLUTE

Rhythm and back are so closely related that you might say: "If back is where you want to go, rhythm is how you get there." That isn't the only thing rhythm does, of course, but it's certainly one of its most important results.

The plain fact is that when you go up to bat, you've got to *move*. You can't get up there and just stand dead still, not if you want to hit consistently and to the maximum of your ability. This movement or rhythm can take many forms, and it varies greatly with the individual. Some guys get up to the plate and almost seem to be rocking back and forth, going forward toward the pitcher and then back toward the catcher. With others the movement is so subtle, so close to an internal weight shift, that you can't see it unless you're standing right behind them. But all good hitters have it. Every one of them has some form of rhythm.

The reasons why rhythm helps you get your weight back and then bring it forward can be found in elementary physics. But there's no need to get that technical. All you have to do is think of a tennis player waiting for his opponent to return the ball. The player waiting for the return doesn't stand there like a stone. He hunches down, grabs his racket with both hands, and shifts from foot to foot so he'll be ready to move when the ball comes across the net.

It's the same thing in hitting. By developing a rhythm when you're in your stance waiting for the pitch, you get ready to move when the ball arrives. You've already overcome some of your body's inertia, and you've already got some momentum. So your weight shift at the critical time is much easier and much more effective.

Rhythm also helps you achieve the proper balance. It's hard to move if your weight is back on your heels. Rhythm forces you to literally stay on your toes. A good rhythm can also eliminate tension, since if you're moving, your muscles can't lock themselves into a tense, inflexible position.

RITUALS AND ROUTINES

As I mentioned earlier, it's not always easy to get a player to incorporate rhythm and back in his stance. And putting these into yours may not be easy either. We're all creatures of habit and we all tend to prefer what's comfortable and familiar to things that are new and unknown. It took Lou Piniella nearly a season to get completely comfortable after we agreed he should move his feet more in the stance. But he stuck with it because he knew it was right, and it's paid big dividends.

I urge you to do the same. Experiment during batting practice with different kinds of movement until you find a style that's right for you. Make it a permanent part of your stance and make a mental commitment to stay with it. You may have to alter things here and there or make some minor adjustments as time goes on. But don't be discouraged if you go to the plate and make out or if you're not in the groove after one at-bat. It takes time, patience, and practice to unlearn bad habits and replace them with something new and better. And that applies to coaches as well as players.

One thing that will almost certainly help is the deliberate development of a little 1-2-3 ritual or routine to be gone through in sequence each

Taking several good practice swings is an excellent way to get your in-stance rhythm started. In photo 4-3 George Brett has just finished a practice swing and in succeeding photos is shown in the process of bringing the bat back and into position as he goes into his stance. Notice how his weight shifts forward in photo 4-4, causing his back foot to come up. As the process continues, notice

how George shifts his weight back, particularly in photo 4-8, where his front foot comes up.

He finishes in photo 4-10 with his bat in position and most of his weight on his back leg. From here the rhythm continues as a more or less internal shifting of weight forward and back, forward and back.

time you step up to the plate. As you already know, this can be important in getting your bat into the correct position when you take your stance. But it's also a good way to get your rhythm going.

Watch Bobby Murcer sometime. You'll see him start with his front foot wide and move it in a bit as he takes his first practice swing. On the second swing he moves the foot in closer, and closer still on the third. As he finishes that third swing, his feet are in position, his bat is headed for the correct spot, and his weight is moving back onto his rear leg to begin his in-stance rhythm.

Bobby does this every time he bats. It's his personal routine, and he's found it invaluable. I'd recommend something similar to just about anybody. Alter it to suit your own style, but be sure to include some good, healthy practice swings. Swinging the bat just as you would if hitting a ball works best. I don't think there's any point to swinging the bat like a golf club or in any way other than you will when hitting an actual pitch. Smooth, rhythmical practice swings will help you get into the groove. They'll force you up on to your toes for good balance and help you get your weight-shift rhythm started.

The most unusual method of putting rhythm into a player's stance I ever saw was devised by a Little League coach in Adelaide, Australia. Most Australian kids play cricket, but there's a hard core of dedicated baseball enthusiasts that's growing larger every year as the general popularity of the sport increases. Australian coaches frequently visit major-league training camps, and when a group of them once invited me to spend six weeks giving clinics in their country I was happy to accept.

In Adelaide I watched a particularly well-organized and well-coached Little League team taking batting practice, and I've got to say, I didn't believe what I saw. These were ten-year-old kids, and they were executing what the coach called a "quick step." Before the pitcher threw. each batter would take a stride. Then as the pitcher threw, they'd come back and stride again in the normal way.

It seemed really strange until I thought about it a bit and watched some more. The quick step, as it turned out, was their in-stance movement. It was the coach's way of making sure his players moved and had rhythm, and I think he was onto something, for I saw it work.

A technique like that could probably only be invented in a country that doesn't have a strong baseball tradition. Through no fault of their own, most kids over there don't have much of a background in baseball, and that presents special challenges to anyone trying to coach them. But it also produces certain benefits. Because they have very few preconceptions, most players are completely receptive.

With limited sources of baseball information and with no major-league players to copy, about all most of them knew was that you pick up a bat and try to hit the ball and it's hard as hell to do. They'd stand there at the plate as rigid as a rock and be completely useless. They couldn't hit at all. The key that seemed to work with them was: "Keep moving your feet." The minute you told them to move the bat and move their feet, they all began to do much better.

The younger kids, the ones from seven to fifteen, picked it up very quickly. I could say, "Hey, do what I do," and show them what I wanted. They'd do it and be swinging pretty well right from the start. A lot of the older kids, though, had more trouble adjusting. What seemed to work best with them was telling them to raise each heel as they moved the bat in the stance. This gave them the necessary rhythm and made their weight shift more effective.

YOU HIT OFF YOUR FRONT LEG

Any of these techniques may work for you, and it might be a good idea to try them in practice. In this country, though, you've got to do something that most Australian players don't have to worry much about. You've got to be especially careful to look at hitting with an open mind. The long baseball tradition here has inadvertently produced a number of red herrings in the form of misleading tips and misinformed rules of thumb. The one about "top hand" and the one about aligning your knuckles in the grip are two examples. Another is the rule stating, "You hit off your back leg."

In this photo George has shifted his weight forward to the point where it's "on top" of his front leg. Notice the nearly straight line formed by his front leg, right hip, and right shoulder. This is a very workable position, though I'd hesitate to call it "perfect," because that term doesn't apply here. However, this is the position I ask players to shoot for, since it emphasizes the importance of coming forward.

These photos show several degrees of being "against" your front leg, as opposed to being "on top." Each player has to find the position that works best for him, but it's best to avoid extremes like those shown in photos 4-14 and 4-15.

Like so many rules, both good and bad, this one gets parroted by players, coaches, and even textbooks without anyone ever once stopping to think about what it really means. As proof, you have only to ask someone who preaches "back leg" if he also believes there must be a forward weight shift during the swing. I guarantee you he'll say "yes." It doesn't make any sense!

Yet fifteen years ago all you ever heard was, "You've got to hit off your back leg." I tried to work it out, but I couldn't see any way to do it. So I decided then and there to believe my eyes and not my ears, and it's saved me a lot of grief.

I think part of the problem is that a lot of people aren't sure exactly what happens when a hitter swings. They aren't sure what the sequence is. But having studied films, tapes, and live batters for years, there just isn't any doubt in my mind that you hit from a firm, rigid back side to a firm, rigid front side—that is, you transfer the weight forward so that you hit from your *front* leg, not your back leg. This is an Absolute.

At the point of contact, all good hitters have a front side that's as stiff and rigid as a piece of oak planking. As they follow through they may relax their front leg or flip the bat over their shoulder or do something else. But at the moment of truth, they're all right there, with the same stiff front side.

Here are two examples of extremes in the opposite direction. Photo 4-16 shows a position a little forward of "on top," but it's still very workable. The position shown in photo 4-17 is even more extreme and probably should be avoided by most players.

4-16

4-17

A firm front leg is your "base of operations." It gives you the kind of foundation you need to swing the bat and hit a ball coming in at close to ninety miles per hour. You know you've got to shift your weight. Well, your front leg is where you shift it to.

I like to say that you shift your weight to a point where it's "on top" of your front leg because it emphasizes the fact that the player must come forward, even though I know some players will end up more "against." It's all a question of degree, and there really isn't much difference between "on" and "against." The key point is that you've got to come forward to a stiff front side to hit the ball.

WHEN DOES THE STRIDE BEGIN?

"When does the stride begin?" is a question everybody asks. And to that I can confidently reply, "Who knows?" No, I'm serious. Every batter has his own style and rhythm, and each commits himself a little differently. The thing I do know is that all good hitters react when the ball is still in the pitcher's hand.

A couple of years ago I filmed an entire game with a mirror-and-camera setup that let me see both the batter and the pitcher at the same time. This produced a split-screen image and made it clear that every batter begins to react when the pitcher has his arm almost completely extended, just before he releases the ball.

But it also showed that everyone reacts differently. If at the key moment the batter moved his upper body either up or forward, instead of starting to stride with his foot, he had a poor swing. If his first reaction was to move back and then move his front foot forward (without moving his body in that direction at the same time), his swing was generally pretty good.

With practice I think each batter determines his own best moment of reaction. It's something that, after you've faced enough pitchers and batting machines, you develop and learn to adjust naturally. Far more important is the *kind* of reaction you initiate. I think the evidence shows that moving back as part of your rhythm and then striding forward with your front foot without bringing the bulk of your body along work best.

This brings up another very important point. And that is that a hitter must step first and swing second. The line that divides these two actions isn't always obvious in real time since everything happens so fast. But slow it down electronically and it becomes clear as day. Successful hitters always step to swing; they don't try to do both at the same time. Players who combine the two actions invariably "bring their hands with them" when they swing—that is, they begin to uncoil their upper bodies and start their hands swinging the bat at the same time they are striding forward. That reduces both their power and their ability to make contact with the ball.

When you think about it, stepping first and swinging second is the only logical way to do things. As I said earlier, your front leg is your foundation. Only after it is firm and securely positioned can you hope to move the rest of your body effectively. Stepping and swinging at the same time is like trying to put up the first floor of a house while you're still digging the basement. It doesn't make sense.

AN AGGRESSIVE STRIDE

The problem of how far to stride can be one of the more troubling questions in hitting, especially for baseball coaches. Often it creates a dilemma, forcing a coach to choose between sound mechanics and the equally essential attitude of aggressiveness on the part of the batter. You see, although the actual feet-and-inches distance of the stride is determined by the player's body type, generally speaking, a relatively short stride provides better balance, timing, and control. Yet the minute you teach it, you risk taking away some of the batter's aggressiveness.

Successful hitters always step first and then swing. The first reaction is to shift your weight back (4-18). Then start the stride by picking up your front foot and shifting your weight forward (4-19). The bat goes into the launching position as the front foot hits to give you a firm foundation (4-20). Then you swing.

To be a good hitter you have to make a positive, aggressive motion back at the pitcher. You've got to dig toward him, attack back at him. That's an Absolute that good hitters have always followed, but it's something you don't see nearly enough of in your average ballplayer.

I think it's possible that this lack of aggressiveness is a habit a player forms early in his career, maybe even before he enters his teens. In Little League, for example, it's usually the big, strong, overgrown kid who gets chosen to be the pitcher. Team managers put him on the mound and, facing smaller players who haven't reached their growth spurt yet and who may be a little uncoordinated, he just dominates the whole game.

The big guy strikes out everybody and throws the fear of the Lord into every batter who walks up there. Team competition is intense, so the manager tells his hitters, "Take. Try to get a base on balls. Don't swing." That kind of thing has led to a whole generation of takers, batters who have lost their aggressiveness before they've even begun.

A strong youngster or one with intense desire can overcome this. He can develop aggressiveness in spite of early habits. But the "take" brand of coaching can drive a less capable kid into a shell. He can't go compete anyplace where he's got to hit the ball. This may be why an average boy may not like to play baseball by the time he gets to high school.

I'm a firm believer that you've got to plan to swing at every pitch. You get ready for it. You get into position. And you swing until your mind tells you it's a ball. As a coach it's crucial to just get your batters to swing. Often this can be done best by either pitching yourself or by using a pitching machine, since in both cases the element of fear will be reduced or eliminated, allowing your batters to be more aggressive.

So you can see why I hesitate to teach "short stride." Even though I know that it might be beneficial for a batter to have a shorter stride, I've yet to find a way to cut down the distance and still maintain the batter's aggressiveness.

Nor do I teach "long stride," per se. A long stride limits you to areas, especially when the ball's inside. You can hit the ball the other way (to the opposite field) with a long stride and you can hit it straight back through the box. But you can't pull, at least not intentionally. Telling a batter to pull and take a long stride causes him to lose extension and to shorten his swing awkwardly. And since his reaction must be quicker, it also builds up tension.

However, a long-stride batter *can* pull if he doesn't deliberately try to. I know it's a paradox, but if the batter concentrates on taking a rhythmical, graceful, positive swing he has a much better chance of pulling the ball than if he goes up there thinking "Pull, pull, pull."

Instead of worrying about whether a batter's stride is too long or too short, I try to get him to focus on attacking the ball. The stride then usually takes care of itself. However, in younger players especially, this

This is a good example of striding with the front toe closed. You'll notice that the toe has opened a little, as it must. It's no longer pointing straight ahead (closed), as it was in the stance. By thinking "closed toe," you're able to keep your hips from opening too soon. Notice that only now, at the "moment of contact," does George begin to open his hips.

approach often leads to criticism for "lunging," and to coaches' misguided attempts to stop it, which, of course, reduce aggressiveness.

Admittedly, a lunge is not good. It causes the upper body to come too far forward too fast. Yet there *is* something of a lunge in the stride and weight shift. Again, there's a fine line between a lunge and an aggressive attack. The main difference is that a lunge is not a balanced move. An attack may look similar, but it's really a balanced, coordinated action in which the body comes forward as the bat goes into the launching position. I think coaches would get better results in most cases if they worried less about lunging and more about attacking the ball correctly.

STRIDE WITH THE FRONT TOE CLOSED

In discussing rhythm, weight shift, and stride, we've talked a lot about feet and the vital role they play. So maybe it's only fitting to conclude with some final points on feet, or more specifically, on toes. The position of the toes on your front foot and the toes on your back foot are like bookends marking the beginning and the end of the swing.

When you begin the stride, it's important to step with your front-shoe toe closed—that is, with the toes on your front foot pointing straight ahead, just as they do in your preparatory, parallel stance. If you stride with your front toe open (pointing out into the infield), you'll cause your front hip to open too soon. That means you'll be swinging with your front hip already open, and that has the effect of squandering your power.

Turning your hips outward is the trigger that brings your shoulders and upper body around and thus is one of the keys to putting the body's power into the ball. Ideally, a batter should start the swing from a firm

The back foot should come up so that the toes are pointing directly into the ground at the completion of the swing. If this doesn't happen, it's a sure sign of a poor weight shift.

front side, with hips closed. Then, at the moment of contact, whip the hips around. This way, the power of the hips is applied to the ball at the same moment that the power of the arms is at its peak. All the power of the body is concentrated on the same spot at the same time.

If you open your hips too soon, you'll have already spent much of their power before you make contact with the ball. What's more, because of the twisting effect of opening your hips, your upper body will not be in the best position to bring the bat ahead to the target. You'll have difficulty keeping your eye on the ball, among other problems.

All of this adds up to a pretty powerful argument for the Absolute of stepping with your front-shoe toe closed. That at least is how you should think of it when beginning your stride. In reality, the front toe *will* open a little. It has to. But if you go up to the plate thinking in those terms, you'll probably open your toe too much. By thinking "closed toe," you'll have a much better chance of striding with just the right degree of openness.

Finally, there's the matter of the back toes. Quite simply, the back foot should come up so that the toes are pointing directly into the ground at the completion of the swing. How far up is right for you may be another matter of degree. But I know that the distance the back heel comes up off the ground is a pretty accurate measure of the effectiveness of your weight shift and pivot.

To hit the ball hard, you've got to shift your weight and you've got to pivot to open your hips at the correct moment. You can't do these things properly if you don't raise your back foot close to where the toes are pointing straight down. When you concentrate on rhythm, weight shift, and other major points, the back-shoe toe usually takes care of itself.

However, when a player's having trouble with this, there's one suggestion I've found that works particularly well. I tell him to take his top hand off the bat after hitting the ball. Everything in the hitting swing is intimately connected. By removing the top hand, the player eliminates the main barrier that's been preventing him from shifting his weight effectively and hampering his body's pivot and momentum. With the top hand off, the back foot almost always comes up to the spot it should.

HITTER ANALYSIS

HENRY AARON
HEIGHT: 6 feet
WEIGHT: 180 pounds
AVERAGE (lifetime): .305

Henry Aaron has always raised one of those fascinating "What if?" questions that makes baseball so interesting both on and off the field. Here was a man who became the most successful home-run hitter in baseball. Yet he probably also had the ability to hit .400 more times than anyone else in the history of the sport. What if he'd set that as his goal? Could he have done it? Would his club have benefited more from the hits than the homers? Who knows?

I do know that Henry Aaron was the greatest example I've ever seen of a tension-free preparatory stance and that he had a graceful, fluid, almost effortless way of attacking the ball. There were a lot of reasons for his success. He made a habit of watching the ball, for instance. And he didn't allow himself to get tense.

But the most outstanding characteristic of Aaron's swing, I feel, was his tremendous weight shift. (You can see just the beginning of it as he gets ready to stride in this picture.) I played with him in both Milwaukee and Atlanta, and had the opportunity to observe his style close up for a long period of time. Hank would do the same things in every at-bat. But even though it was all there in front of me, it somehow didn't stick right away. It was only by watching him day after day that I began to realize what set him apart.

Aaron was one of the first players I noticed who clearly went back to go forward to hit off a firm, rigid front leg. Watching him with this thought in mind, the importance of a forward weight shift became obvious. After that I began to look at other successful hitters and noticing variations of the same thing.

There used to be a stigma attached to front-leg hitting, for the general opinion was that you couldn't be a front-foot hitter and still hit home runs. Yet few players had a more clearly defined forward weight shift than Henry Aaron, and as everyone knows, nobody hit more home runs. So I think that's one incorrect opinion that can safely be laid to rest.

Rhythm, Weight Shift, and Stride

83

HITTER ANALYSIS

JACK CLARK
HEIGHT: 6 feet, 3 inches
WEIGHT: 205 pounds
AVERAGE (1985): .281

Of the 1985 National League Champion St. Louis Cardinals, their twenty-one-game-winning pitcher Joaquin Andular said, "We've got two power hitters on this team. Jack Clark and me." He wasn't kidding. Though Tommy Herr knocked in over 100 runs and Willie McGee won the batting title, it was Clark who provided the bulk of the power for a team that won the pennant primarily because of speed and defense.

In 1984 Jack was well on his way to a banner year with the San Francisco Giants when a knee injury required surgery and limited his appearances to only fifty-seven games. Still, he managed 11 home runs and batted .320. In 1985, after being traded to the Cards in the off-season, he took up where he left off the year before, banging out 22 round-trippers, despite the fact that he was out for five weeks with a rib-cage injury.

This is a great shot of Jack hitting through the ball, something he does as well as anyone. He puts his head down when he swings, one of the Absolutes. This enables him to see the ball for a longer period of time, thus allowing him to keep his eye on the ball and not pull away.

Jack also does something else very well: he strides in with his front toe closed, which keeps his hips from opening up too soon. If the hips open up too early, a lot of power is lost and you are pulled out of hitting position. In this photo, you can see that Jack's front foot was almost closed down when he planted it, and then it rolls over as he swings, much as a golfer's.

Another thing that Jack does so well is, despite the fact that he's a power hitter, use the entire field to hit in, hitting the ball where it's pitched, rather than always trying to pull it to his power field.

HITTER ANALYSIS

WILLIE MAYS
HEIGHT: 5 feet, 10½ inches
WEIGHT: 170 pounds
AVERAGE (lifetime): .302

Willie Mays ranks seventh in lifetime hits (3,283), fourth in runs scored (2,062) behind Cobb, Aaron, and Ruth, and third in home runs (660) behind only Aaron and Ruth. Willie was truly one of the game's exceptional players. He had great talent, and, although I think the dis-

cipline of his head could probably have been better, good mechanics. He had excellent arm extension. He would go to the ball, and he used the whole field to hit in.

I think the thing I'll always remember about Willie was his sheer aggressiveness. The way Willie Mays attacked the ball was just unreal. He coiled; he was always moving; and at the last minute he came way back toward the catcher and then forward simply to explode at the ball.

His weight shift was tremendous. Like Henry Aaron, Willie Mays always got back to go forward, which is one of the reasons why both men rank so high in lifetime records of hits, runs, and home runs.

HITTER ANALYSIS

DAVE PARKER
HEIGHT: 6 feet, 5 inches
WEIGHT: 230 pounds
AVERAGE (1979): .310

I don't know an awful lot about Dave Parker. But I did see him at an exhibition game one spring several years ago. I remember him as a big, gangling kid who was very graceful with a bat in his hands. Since that time he's shown himself to be a good outfielder and a good base runner as well as a good hitter—a complete player, in other words, who's possibly one of the top three or four in the National League.

At bat, he combines consistency and power. He uses the whole field to hit in. A good off-speed hitter, his talents have led him to two National League batting titles—in 1977 with .338 and in 1978 with .334— and a .310 average in 1979. A look at this photograph helps explain why he's been so successful.

If you look closely, you'll see that the ball's in the catcher's glove, and judging from where he's holding it, I'd say the ball was away. But even though Parker missed, it was still a good swing. You can see right away that it was tension-free. And you can tell from the position of the back leg, among other things, that the weight shift was good. Notice also that the front toe is opened just the right amount. Judging from his upper-body position, I'd say that he probably also put his head down to watch the ball.

Dave Parker uses a closed stance and he holds his bat up high. But he takes deliberate care to set up his stance properly each time. All in all, I think his mechanics are good for a big man.

Wide World

HITTER ANALYSIS

MICKEY MANTLE
HEIGHT: 5 feet, 11½ inches
WEIGHT: 195 pounds
AVERAGE (lifetime): .298

Mickey Mantle could do it all. Hit, run, field, throw—you name it. But it was with a bat in his hands that the sheer ability of the man shone most brightly. And this picture from 1956 tells a lot about the qualities that made him so good.

To begin with, his bat position is superb. This shot was taken just after his front foot hit, and as you can see, Mickey's bat is exactly where

it should be—right in the launching position. There's no doubt about it: He's going to hit a good pitch.

The photo also shows the start of a great weight shift. Mantle never fooled around. He always attacked the ball and always made a positive, aggressive motion back at the pitcher.

Which is why it's possible to pass over the fact that his stride was a mite too long. His front-toe position here is excellent. It's opened just the right amount. And although his stride is wider than ideal mechanics would dictate, I'm not sure in this case that it could have been shortened up without sacrificing aggressiveness. As long as everything was working well, which it did most of the time, Mantle could take that big step and get away with it.

Rhythm, Weight Shift, and Stride

91

5
YOUR HEAD GOES DOWN WHEN YOU SWING

If I could tell Little League and other young players only one thing that would improve their hitting it would be this: *Your head goes down when you swing.* At the moment of contact, the bat should be straight out in front of you, your arms should be fully extended, and your head should be *down*, eyes on the ball. This is an Absolute, and all the other Absolutes —rhythm, balance, lack of tension, etc.—work together to make it possible.

The simple fact is that good hitters see the ball longer than poor hitters. Your mechanics can be good, and your swing can be good. But if you don't see the ball, you're not going to hit it. Even if the rest of your mechanics are rotten, if your head goes down when you swing, you can still have a degree of success.

As a baseball player, you've probably heard coaches say, "Don't move your head," or you've heard them talk about the "discipline of the head." These terms and phrases refer to the same thing. But while they're both good things to say, the first is negative (a "don't" instead of a "do") and the second isn't very descriptive. As a coach I've found that positive instructions that give a player specific details about what he should do are the most effective. That's why I told my own son what I'm telling you: "Whenever you swing the bat, put your head down and watch the ball."

If you think that sounds like the old phrase, "Keep your eye on the ball," you're absolutely right. Both instructions refer to the same thing. Yet the more familiar phrase has been used so often, not just in baseball but in other areas of life as well, that nobody seems to know what it means anymore. Ballplayers especially aren't aware of how critical it is to see the ball or what they've got to do to make it possible.

I speak from experience. If there were one thing I could do over in my whole career it would be to bat with my head down and my eyes on the ball. Like most players, I heard all of the rules of thumb and parroted the phrases from my coaches. I was told to keep my eye on the ball. I tried and thought that that was what I was doing. But I now know that I really didn't understand what it meant. It wasn't until I began really to study hitting at Kansas City's baseball academy in Sarasota that I realized how critical watching the ball is and what you've got to do to accomplish it. If I'd known earlier, I'd have been a much better hitter.

WHY IT'S SO IMPORTANT

Putting your head down when you swing serves at least two purposes, one rather obvious, the other not so obvious. Let's take the less obvious one first.

In every sport or physical activity, your head leads your body. Wherever you point or turn your head, the rest of you is sure to follow. That's just the way the human body is set up.

In baseball you can probably see this best when you throw a ball. If you turn your head to one side while you're in the act of throwing, what happens? Your head turns, causing your shoulders to turn, which causes your throwing arm to lag along behind. If you keep your head and shoulders square and pointed at your target, your throwing arm goes nearly straight back and forward to release the ball. But if you turn your head while you're bringing that arm forward, you force it to curve around as it approaches the point of release. You force it to lag behind. What's more, you make it impossible to throw on target.

The same thing can happen in hitting, only here you're dealing with a bat instead of your throwing arm. If you turn your head as you swing, you cause the bat to lag behind. That not only reduces your power, it also pulls you off-target, making it impossible to put the bat head on the ball. (A "quick hip," as we'll see in the next chapter, causes similar problems. If you open your front hip, you've got to turn your head outward, causing the bat to lag and making it impossible to watch the ball.)

Your head leads your body. So instead of saying, "Don't move your head," I think it's better to say, "Go on and follow your head. Just be sure to point it in the right direction." In batting, that direction is *down.*

Of course, to get your head into the proper position at the moment of contact, you've got to have it in the proper position in your stance. One easy way I've found to help batters achieve this position concerns what they can see with each eye. Close the eye nearer the pitcher or cover it with your hand. Then turn your head back toward the catcher until you can just see the pitcher with your other eye. To be sure you're doing it correctly, you might want to turn your head so far back that you can't see the pitcher with your open eye and then slowly turn it forward, stopping just at the point where the pitcher comes into view. This will put your head in exactly the right starting position.

Once you've got that position, do your best to keep it. You can turn your eyes to watch the pitcher and you can turn your head a very small amount to follow the ball. But the minute your head comes up or turns very much, you've lost it. Think: "*Down. My head goes down when I swing,*" keep your eyes open, and concentrate on watching the ball for as long as you possibly can.

Allowing you to watch the ball is the second and more obvious purpose of putting your head down. If your head is anyplace else but down, aimed directly at the spot where the ball and bat will make contact, you're not going to see the ball, and you're not going to hit it.

Nothing could be simpler than that, unless it's the fact that if you're going to see the ball, you've got to have your eyes open. But unfortunately, that's not as easy as it sounds. Every now and then you'll see one of those photos in the newspaper that are worth ten thousand words. You'll see a batter with his head down, his arms fully extended, and his eyes *wide open* at the point of contact.

This is not a natural reaction, any more than keeping your eyes from blinking when you're driving a nail with a hammer is a natural reaction. In fact, it's exactly the opposite. For protection, the human body has a number of involuntary reflexes. When you fall, you automatically shoot your hands out to catch yourself. And when you hit a ball with a bat, you automatically close your eyes—*unless* you've trained yourself to keep them open. The chances are that any batter you see with his eyes open at the point of contact has done just that.

Now, I think it can't be done all the time. Sometimes you're going to blink. And sometimes you may flinch. But by simply trying to watch the ball as long as possible, you'll greatly improve your chances of hitting it. If your head's down and your eyes are open up to a fraction of a second before impact, even if you blink, you'll have seen the ball longer than most and be more likely to hit it.

I've got to say, though, that the great hitters of the past usually didn't blink. They all watched the ball from start to finish. And they did it by deliberately overcoming their tendency to blink at the moment of contact.

The reason they could do this was more than just a deliberately desensitized blink reaction, however. It was and is related to everything else

Here's a closer look at where your head should be at the moment of contact. It should be pointed down at the bat as you watch the ball.

If you move your head even this much, you'll pull your body out of position at the critical moment and, as this photo shows, you won't see the ball.

Here George Brett is demonstrating a bad extreme of moving your head. Yet although it's an extreme, this is exactly what a lot of young players would see if they could catch themselves in slow motion. Obviously, it's impossible to see the ball if you turn your head like this.

in the swing, all the other Absolutes I've been talking about. For example, to put your head down you've got to move *toward* a ball moving upward of eighty-five miles per hour. If you aren't balanced, you won't be able to do this. You'll be so concerned about protecting yourself that your mind won't let you be positive and aggressive and go back at the pitcher. It's another of those involuntary reactions. Your head will go up, not down. Your body will back away, and you won't be able to see the ball.

The same kind of thing happens if you're tense because you're really

When taking a pitch, *the batter's initial movements are identical to when swinging. The weight is shifted from the rear leg with an aggressive drive toward the pitcher. Concentration is on "seeing the ball."*

Eyes are riveted on the ball and the head in "down." The batter is in position either to continue or to stop the swing.

trying to crush the ball. To do that you'll have to swing exceptionally hard. I'm all for swinging hard. But I also know that the harder you swing, the more you're going to move your head.

If you follow the Absolutes, however, they will all work together to make it easier for you to put your head down and watch the ball all the time. That applies even when you decide not to swing at a ball.

To take a pitch correctly, follow the ball all the way into the catcher's glove. If you rise up or relax when you see it's a ball, you'll relax and break

The decision not to swing has been made, but the head and eyes continue to follow the ball's flight.

As the ball enters the hitting area, the head and eyes remain fixed on its path.

your concentration. Instead, on every pitch, your stride should be there, your hands should be there, your eyes should be on the ball. In other words, you should be all set to swing until the last moment when you decide it's not a strike. And even then you should follow the ball into the catcher's glove.

By approaching it this way, you'll be keyed on that ball for the greatest period of time. You'll always be ready. And, like all good hitters, you'll see the ball longer than a poor hitter.

The ball passes over the plate; the batter has never lost sight of the ball. He has seen the ball continuously from the time it left the pitcher's hand.

HITTER ANALYSIS

JIM RICE
HEIGHT: 6 feet, 2 inches
WEIGHT: 200 pounds
AVERAGE: (1979): .325

Jim Rice represents a highly unusual and highly successful combination of talents and techniques. One of the strongest men playing ball today, he concentrates on hitting the ball and seems to pull more or less without deliberately trying to. He also has tremendous discipline of the head. Look at where his head and eyes are in this picture, for instance. His eyes are clearly on the ball (a barely visible blur at the far right) coming in at about hip level. In a few fractions of a second the ball will be even closer and Jim's head will be down even farther.

You don't find this very often with men of Rice's strength. Strength is fine in football players, but if you ask a football player to swing a bat, you usually find he lacks the necessary flexibility in his upper body to keep his eye on the ball. He moves his head, and his whole upper body tends to move with it. Exceptionally strong baseball players have similar problems, which is why Rice is so unusual.

You can't really see it in this picture, but if you watched Rice play, you'd notice a very dominant top hand. However, you'd also see a good weight shift forward to a rigid front leg in a style similar to Henry Aaron's. In both cases the weight shift and front-foot hitting are ways of compensating. They're what allow Rice to be dominant with his top hand and still be successful.

A player who doesn't get to his front leg before rolling the top hand over couldn't do this. Such players have no weight shift. They tend to collapse their rear legs and back away from the ball at the moment of contact. The only way a top-hand hitter can be successful is by having an extremely good forward weight shift to a firm, rigid front leg, as Jim Rice with 39 home runs in 1979 and an average of .325 has clearly shown.

HITTER ANALYSIS

STEVE GARVEY
HEIGHT: 5 feet, 10 inches
WEIGHT: 192 pounds
AVERAGE (1985): .281

One particular at-bat stands out in my mind whenever I think of Steve Garvey. He was facing Rollie Fingers, one of the best relief pitchers in the game. Garvey took seven or eight damn near perfect swings, but he kept fouling them off. In each one, his weight shift was excellent, his head was down, and he had full extension of his arms.

You don't see one near-perfect swing very often, let alone seven or eight in a row. Yet he couldn't seem to have any success. A lesser player might have just given up and swung at anything simply to get it over with. But not Garvey. A true professional, he realized that any time you've got two human beings facing each other sixty feet, six inches away, things like that can happen. Through it all he kept watching the ball and just trying to hit it. As it was, he eventually got a base hit and so created a happy ending to one of the toughest at-bats I've ever seen.

If Steve had been thinking, "Pull, pull, pull," he wouldn't have watched the ball so well and I think Rollie would have struck him out. Instead he was concentrating on just hitting the ball. That gave him a chance to see it and was largely responsible for his eventual success. In fact, I think it's true of his whole career and the impressive statistics he's been able to rack up.

Steve is a very strong, muscular player, and his swing does not exemplify the graceful, fluid movement that is the ideal. Yet his preparatory movement is very well defined. You really see his feet moving and the rhythm they generate. And he has excellent discipline of the head. His head goes down and he watches the ball whenever he swings. These two characteristics are the main reasons for his success.

Success at the plate runs in streaks sometimes, even if you're "perfect" on each swing. But pitch after pitch in game after game, the guy who can discipline himself to practice the Absolutes—to put his head down, to shift his weight, and so forth—will be successful sooner or later. If your mechanics are good and if your main goal is simply to hit the ball, you'll hit your share of home runs and you'll have a good average to boot. With 28 home runs and an average of .315 in 1979, Steve Garvey illustrates this fact as well as anyone else I know of.

HITTER ANALYSIS

BILLY WILLIAMS
HEIGHT: 6 feet, 1 inch
WEIGHT: 175 pounds
AVERAGE (lifetime): .290

This picture captures two of the most prominent characteristics of Billy Williams' swing—one good and one bad. As you can see, Billy's head is down and his eyes are right on the ball. That's the good feature. The bad one isn't quite so obvious. If you look closely, though, you can see he's got a dominant top hand. If this picture had been taken just a few fractions of a second later, you would see Billy hitting the ball and rolling his left hand over.

This raises an interesting point. I have found that if you can maintain a good discipline of the head—that is, if you always make sure that you put your head down when you swing and watch the ball, you can get away with rolling the top hand. However, I've also found that players with the ability to combine these two techniques successfully are extremely rare.

Clearly Billy Williams had that ability. So too does Jim Rice. Jim compensates for his dominant top hand by having good discipline of the head and by making sure that he gets to his front leg to hit the ball. If he didn't shift his weight properly or if he collapsed his rear leg, he wouldn't be able to hit as well.

Most people don't have this ability, though. And when, as a coach, you see all the problems the top hand causes, you've just got to be prejudiced against it.

Those who remember seeing Williams play will also recall that there was absolutely no tension involved in his swing. His rhythm was superb. He always had his feet moving in perfect tempo while in the stance, which is another reason why his top hand didn't hurt him as much as it would most other players. Yet, although it's only one man's opinion, I think he probably would have ended up with a .320 lifetime average if he hadn't been so top-hand and home-run conscious, particularly later in his career.

HITTER ANALYSIS

AL KALINE
HEIGHT: 6 feet, 1½ inches
WEIGHT: 175 pounds
AVERAGE (lifetime): .297

I played with Al Kaline when we were both just starting out in Detroit, and he always struck me as having a graceful, nonmuscular swing in those days. He won the American League batting title with a .340 average in 1955 when he was only 20 years old. As he got older, though, he got stronger and that may have caused a few problems. But the older he got, the tougher out he became. He had great discipline, for he always knew when he could afford to try for the home run and when the situation dictated that he hit it the other way.

And like all good hitters, he knew the right way to compensate when he made a mistake, which is what you see him doing here. For this to be a good swing, Al would have had to hit the ball more out in front of the plate. As it is, I think he may have been fooled a little on the pitch. When he realized the ball was low and in, he had to go down to get it. And to do that he had to pull his left arm in, making it impossible to get full extension.

The important thing this picture shows, though, is that he compensated the right way. In a similar situation, a less experienced, less successful hitter tends to raise his head and turn his body to get the bat head to the ball. In stop-action photographs he would seem to shy away from the ball. Kaline, on the other hand, still has that positive downward motion with his head. This is tough to maintain when the ball's inside. But it's the right way to compensate when you're fooled on a pitch like this. A successful hitter will always fight to keep his head down and his eye on the ball.

6
THE SWING AND
THE FOLLOW-THROUGH

As the batter, your goal is to hit the baseball as hard and as consistently as your ability allows. That's what all the mechanics we've discussed so far have been leading up to. Yet even if you follow all of those Absolutes absolutely, you can still blow it at the moment of truth—the swing itself—and in the follow-through. The proper stance, stride, rhythm, bat position, and everything else prepare you to swing the bat in a way to ensure maximum force and maximum consistency. But at the last moment, a floppy swing, a quick hip, a bad uppercut, or an awkwardly shortened follow-through can make them all add up to zip.

These and other problems can cause you to err on one side or another. For example, we've all seen the big strong guy with the "home-run swing" who can really wallop the ball—if and when he hits it. He's got maximum force, but no consistency. And he strikes out a lot.

We get a lot of players like that in the big leagues. But we also get the other extreme—the guy who consistently makes contact but produces little in the way of results. Of him some people say, "Well, he doesn't strike out." To which I reply, "Yeah, but he doesn't hit well either." His swing isn't a positive thing. It results in "soft contact" and rarely sends the ball far enough to get on base.

The successful hitter combines *both* qualities. He hits hard and he hits often. He's got power and consistency.

THE DANGER OF BEING TOO "STRONG"

One of the reasons a successful hitter can do this is that he uses a relatively short, compact stroke. A big, long, floppy swing will never produce consistent results. As I mentioned when discussing the stance, the distance the bat head has to travel to get to the impact area is just too great. It requires too much unnecessary movement, reduces the time a player has to see the ball before committing, and allows too many opportunities to make mistakes.

But there's more to it than that. The big swing, and thus the bat position players use to make it possible, are the end results of an attempt to muscle the ball. Big-swinging players try to do it all with the top half of their bodies. They try to use their arms and often powerful biceps to drive the ball.

Yet the evidence shows that the *bottom* half of the body is much more important. If your bottom half works, if you've got a good base, you can always hit the ball hard and far. By using your bottom half correctly, you can transfer the concentrated power of your entire body to hit through the ball.

Unfortunately, many players don't realize this. So they not only rely primarily upon their arms, they also deliberately build up their arm muscles in the mistaken belief that this will increase their power. Well, of course, you want to be strong to hit the ball. And, of course, your arm muscles are important. But often a player will go too far. He'll build up his muscles so much that he loses his fluidity.

A good example of this is Milwaukee shortstop Robin Yount. Robin was a superb young ballplayer in the big leagues at age eighteen. But by the time he turned twenty-two or twenty-three, either from lifting weights or for natural reasons, he had gotten a lot stronger. All of a sudden his swing was muscular. He had lost the smooth, graceful, "just make contact" fluidity that had been largely responsible for his former success.

Robin's case isn't all that unusual. In fact, I think it's a trap a lot of young players fall into. I remember as a young catcher for Baltimore rooming with pitcher Robin Roberts. Roberts was later inducted into the Hall of Fame, and he made a comment one morning when we were on the road in California that I've never forgotten. It was toward the end of the season, a time when the rules permit the clubs to expand their rosters to give their best farm-team prospects a little major-league exposure. The Angels called up a player named Paul Schaal that year. Schaal had had a good season in

Triple-A and his success carried over into his major-league play. With his nice, fluid swing he belted about five home runs over a two-week period.

That particular day Robin was reading the newspaper account of the previous night's game at breakfast. It was a game in which Schaal had hit one of his homers, and Robin read us what Schaal had said to a reporter inquiring about his recent success. "Well, I plan on lifting weights all winter," Schaal said, "I want to get strong so I can hit a lot of home runs."

After he finished reading, Robin took a sip of coffee and as he put the cup down he leaned back and said, "Well, that's one Angel player we won't have to worry about. He won't hit any off us anymore." And to my recollection, he never did.

WHERE THE POWER IS

True power in hitting comes from the lower half of your body. And if you can tap into it through proper mechanics, you can hit the ball a long way, regardless of your size. This is why some smaller players can hit the ball farther than a lot of players who are a lot bigger and "stronger." These smaller players know how to get the most out of their bodies.

In fact, I'd even go so far as to say that smaller players have an advantage that most people don't recognize. Sure, a good big player who follows the Absolutes will hit the ball farther than the little guy who does the same things. But often it's a lot harder for a bigger player to do. Smaller players tend to be quick. And, possibly because their centers of gravity are lower, they usually have better balance. All of this makes it easier for them to put it all together in the proper sequence and get the maximum amount of power out of their bodies.

Where does all this power come from? It comes primarily from the hips, or, more precisely, from the outward rotation of the hips as you shift your weight forward and bring the bat through. But having said that, I've got to add a very strong note of caution. With the possible exception of the misconception about hitting off your back leg, a misunderstanding of the proper use of the hips has caused more hitting problems than anything else in baseball.

To see what I mean, it's important to have the proper sequence clearly in mind. To hit effectively your body must be square at the moment the front foot is planted. Remember, you're building a foundation here, and if you start to swing before you're "set," your foundation will be weak. With your stride complete, you shift your weight as you open your hips (turn them outward) and bring the bat through.

Okay. Now for the problem. As I've said repeatedly, the step and the swing are two distinct movements. There's a fine line between them, but it's there and it's critical. However, the moment you say, "Hips! Hips! Hips!" to a batter, that line disappears. All of a sudden they begin swinging and

The Swing and the Follow-Through

stepping at the same time. They develop what's called a "quick hip," meaning their hips open too soon in the swing, and from then on they don't have a chance. Every unsuccessful hitter in baseball has a quick hip. It's by far the biggest problem in hitting.

When the hip opens too soon, the whole upper body is pulled out of position. The hip turns and brings the torso, shoulders, head, and arms with it—while the bat is *still* in the launching position. It's as though a marksman had everything lined up on the target and someone came along and pushed the barrel of his gun off to one side a split second before he squeezed the trigger.

This is the reason the only ball a poor hitter can hit is the one low and in. That's where his bat is by the time his quick hip has pulled him off target. It's also one of the main reasons quick-hip batters don't see the ball consistently. In turning the whole upper body, the hip causes the head to turn, making it impossible to watch the ball.

These problems are virtually unavoidable once a player begins concentrating on his hips. So I never teach "hips" as such. I would much rather have a player concentrate on striding with his toe closed, on shifting his weight forward to a rigid front side, and on having his head go down when he swings. If the player does these things correctly, the hips will work the way they should automatically.

AVOIDING AN UPPERCUT

You know you've got to have a tension-free, level swing. That's an Absolute. To achieve it, you'll probably have to overcome a tendency to uppercut. Most hitters have a slight uppercut, and according to some people that isn't bad. It's their theory that you want to keep the bat in the same plane as the ball as long as possible. So, since the ball tends to come down at you as it travels from the mound, the thing to do is get your bat into the ball's projected path or trajectory and swing toward it. To do that, you naturally have to swing up.

That makes sense. But my confidence in the accuracy of this theory is considerably undermined by the fact that I've never seen anybody who could make it work. Usually the person who tries to swing a bat that way ends up collapsing his rear leg and opening his hips too quickly. In short, I just don't think you can do it.

Besides, uppercutting can cause an awful lot of harm. For one thing, the uppercutter hits the ball right where it's easiest for his opponents to catch it—high in the air. That's the one area you want to be sure to avoid if you plan to hit safely 30 percent or more of the time. Uppercutting also makes it nearly impossible to get full extension of your arms or complete transfer of your weight into the ball. It puts you in a weak position at the moment of contact and thus robs you of your natural power.

When I was in Australia I heard a term that has stuck with me ever

This is the first move of a bad, uppercutting swing. The stride has been completed, but instead of shifting his weight forward to a firm front leg, the batter has already collapsed his back leg. This has caused his right shoulder to fly out and his hips to open too soon.

Here's the same thing seen from the front. Notice how the collapsing back leg causes the batter to tilt backward and his front shoulder to come up. This tilt puts the hands and bat in a position where an uppercut is unavoidable.

since. The Australians refer to what we call "uppercutting" as "coming from under," and in many ways I think their term does a better job of describing the problem. What happens is this. As the batter begins to swing, he collapses his rear leg. This screws up his weight shift and, because both legs are attached to the same set of hips, causes the front hip to turn outward, opening prematurely. And, since he no longer has any rear support, his weight naturally tilts backward, causing the front of his shoulder to come up. That brings the hands and the bat down to a spot where they can't work effectively.

This whole "shin bone's connected to the knee bone" type of chain reaction happens very quickly. But its end result is to put the batter in a position where he's got to struggle to get the bat on the ball. With his hands and bat brought low by his collapsing rear leg, all the batter can do is swing up at the ball or "come from under." Consequently, at the moment of contact the batter's arms are out in front of him while his upper body is bent back *away* from the ball. In freeze-frame photographs of uppercutting

The Swing and the Follow-Through

batters it almost looks as if the players felt the ball was white hot and are leaning back to avoid the heat as they poke at it with their bats.

The collapsing back leg is the most obvious cause of the problem. But actually it, too, is the effect of something else. The ultimate cause of uppercutting is improper weight shift. If you tell a player, as many have been told, that you hit off your back foot, you seal his fate as an uppercutting hitter.

In order to hit off your back foot, you've got to keep your weight on your back leg. Yet as you stride and swing, the whole motion of your body is forward. Trying to keep your weight on the back leg during this process puts the leg in a very weak position. So it buckles. Basically, you end up collapsing your back leg in order to hit off it.

Clearly the solution lies in a proper forward weight shift to the front leg. If you follow the Absolute about hitting from a firm front side, you make it virtually impossible to "come from under." To see what I mean, try it yourself in slow motion.

Take your stance and your stride. Then slowly swing the bat as you deliberately shift your weight forward. Stop just as you approach the point of contact. Your weight's on your front leg. Your arms are extended, and your head is down to watch the ball. Now just try to uppercut. You'll find that you can't. Your own body blocks you, making it impossible to "come from under" with the bat. That's why telling a player to shift his weight forward and to get off his back leg is such a great cure for an uppercut.

GETTING ON TOP OF THE BALL

But there's something else. To produce a level swing, you also have to get on top of the ball by swinging down at it. That may sound strange, but it's really another case of aiming at an extreme in order to reach an ideal middle point. Even with the proper weight shift, many hitters still have a tendency toward a slight uppercut, which, as long as it remains slight, isn't all that bad. In fact, it's possible that in the perfect swing you do have a slight uppercut. The problems occur when the uppercut is an extreme loop. That's what you want to stay away from, and getting on top of the ball by swinging down is usually a good way to counteract this tendency. Ideally, the two motions will cancel each other out, and result in a *level* swing.

Critics may say, "That's all well and good, but by swinging down at the ball you're going to ground out. You're better off trying to put the ball in the air, because if you hit enough fly balls, you're going to hit a bunch of home runs." Well, you can ground out swinging up at the ball, too. And as for fly balls, that's the worst kind of ball you can hit.

Look, if you've got a level swing and you hit the ball perfectly, you'll hit a line drive. But you're not always going to hit it perfectly, so which side would you rather err on—hitting the ball up or hitting it down? Where do you have the better chance of getting a base hit? If you swing up and you make a mistake, you're going to loft the ball. That often makes it so easy to catch that you might just as well have handed the ball to your opponent. That would produce the same result and have saved you both a lot of trouble.

But if you get on top of the ball and fall short of perfection, you're going to hit a ground ball. And as any fielder knows, the catching or handling of this animal is a much less certain proposition. Hit a fly ball and you're probably a goner. But hit a ground ball and at least you've got a chance.

SWINGING "INSIDE/OUT"

So far I've said nothing about the wrists and how to use them in the swing. This isn't because they aren't important; it's just that they aren't as important as most people think. The wrists must be strong, but they're not a *primary* source of power. They're more important in controlling and directing power than they are in creating it. Thus I think the old standby phrase "wrist popping" may be an overworked expression.

When you swing, your hands should lead the bat head. If you could look down on a batter from directly overhead and watch his swing in slow motion, you would see that up until the point of contact his hands are always closer to the pitcher than the end of the bat is. At the point of contact, the wrists whip the bat into the ball. This is called swinging "inside/out." Technically, all swings fit into this category, and the wrists are crucial to the process. Swinging inside/out makes it possible to hit the ball hard, particularly compared to bringing your hands down and trying to push the bat out and into the ball.

It's that key moment where the wrists direct the bat and the body's force toward the ball that's responsible for the popularity of the phrase "wrist popping." I suppose that phrase is all right, but as a coach and instructor I prefer something more descriptive. I think it's better to tell a player to throw the bat head at the ball. *Let the bat do what it was designed to do.* Rather than trying to muscle it, just start the bat and let it swing. Try for a smooth, graceful, pendulum movement.

This brings up an interesting point, by the way. In professional baseball, sportswriters' catch phrases can stick to a player like glue. Early on, someone once described the great Henry Aaron as a "wrist hitter." The phrase stuck, and for the next fifteen years that was the main characteristic of his hitting style everyone talked about, whether it was accurate or not. My son Charley is in his teens, and he's a pretty good player and student of the game. A while back, when we were talking about baseball greats, Charley said, "Yeah, Henry Aaron was a real wrist hitter. He was super."

Well, he was super, but I'm not so sure he was a wrist hitter. I saw Henry play several times, and the most outstanding feature of his hitting style was actually the way he got his body moving. His weight shift was fantastic, certainly one of the best the game has ever seen. It's true that toward the end of his career, when he was going for the home-run record and trying to hit a homer every time up, he did use his wrists a lot. But in the early sixties when he was building his reputation, that wasn't the case. At that time, whenever he needed a base hit, you'd see him take his top hand off the bat and just try to hit the ball.

I was so glad that of all the players Henry Aaron should be the one to hit more home runs than any other person in baseball, for I daresay he hit at least half of them with his back heel raised, toes pointing down at the ground, indicating a superb weight shift. It's so clear in the photos taken at the time. There's no doubt about it: Henry hit off a firm front leg. He was one player who definitely knew the secret of going back to go forward, and he exploited it fully.

THE POWER POSITION

The old-timers used to say that you made contact with the ball when it was directly over the plate. And I think there are probably a lot of people who still believe that. But that's not the way to do it, for a variety of reasons.

First of all, the farther back from the front of the plate you hit the ball, the greater the chance that it will go foul. And, if it's a breaking pitch, you'll have to contend with more break. To keep the ball fair and to nail it before it really begins to break, you've got to hit it out in front of the plate.

More importantly, however, making contact out in front lets you put the meat of the bat on the ball. You see, there's really only one optimum position in which to make contact with the ball, and that's when the bat, the ball, and your body are all in the same plane.

Picture it for a moment. See yourself in slow motion as you stride, shift your weight forward, swing the bat, and begin to open your hip. Right when you get to the point where your arms are fully extended and your head is down—right at the point of contact—freeze the action. At that point, your bat and body are in the same vertical plane. Indeed, if the grounds crew were to wheel out a gigantic panel of glass and place it vertically so that one end was up against your front foot and the other touched the tip of your bat, there wouldn't be much of a gap in between. That glass plane represents the vertical plane I'm talking about.

This is your power spot. All of the other things you have done, from planting your feet to swinging the bat, have been aimed at bringing you to this point. If you took away the glass panel, imagined a ball touching the fat part of the bat, and then let your mental film run on at normal speed, you'd hear the crack of contact and see the ball flying away.

As you may have noticed, this power spot or optimum position is definitely not directly above home plate. Because of the way your hips open, the way your upper body turns, and the need for full arm extension, the spot must be out in front of the plate.

But what if, because of the game situation, the pitcher, or for some other reason, you want to hit the ball a little later—after it's crossed the front boundary of the plate? The answer is simple and vital. If you want to hit the ball at a different spot, you *don't* do it by tampering with your stance or swing. You do it by changing your starting position in the box or your position relative to the plate and swing just as you always do.

Or think of it another way. The key thing in hitting is to get your bat and body to your power position where everything's in the same plane. That position is always the same as far as your bat and body are concerned. But you can change where it occurs in relation to the plate. All you have to do is decide upon your target spot and work backward. That will tell you where you've got to begin to end up where you want to be.

HITTING THROUGH THE BALL

The follow-through is an essential part of almost every sport. Tennis, golf, discus throwing—you name it. Yet surprisingly it doesn't get nearly the emphasis it deserves in baseball. There are many baseball players who simply don't realize how important it is.

When you hit, you've got to extend your arms completely. You've got to hit *through* the ball. This is an Absolute. If you quit at the point of contact, the ball won't go anywhere. And if you don't drive the ball, if you don't follow through, everything you've done up to that point will be wasted. After all, you can make consistent contact yet just as consistently fail to get on base. I know a number of players in that boat, and the problem with all of them is that they don't get extended and don't hit through the ball.

Now, as a coach, how do you get that across? And as a player, what approach or explanation will do it for you? All coaches (the good ones, anyway) are searching for key phrases or bits of instruction that will hit a responsive chord in their players. Or I should say "player," since with each individual the search begins anew. Each person's different, but we all need goals to aim at or images to focus our efforts on.

For some, thinking of hitting through the ball will produce a good follow-through. Others may do better thinking of their weight shift, of getting full extension, or of throwing the bat head at the ball. The exact image or focal point doesn't matter that much. The critical thing is to be aware of how important the follow-through is and to make sure that it's executed completely every time you swing.

Of course, some players have the opposite problem. They put entirely too much emphasis upon the follow-through, usually more out of concern about how they look than because of an awareness of how best to drive the ball. Once when I was with Kansas City, we had a player who hit .300 one year. He had a sound stance and a good swing and looked to have a solid future with the club.

When I saw him in spring training the following year, though, it was immediately clear that something had gone wrong. The boy had lengthened his swing and was taking a cut so powerful that the pitcher could probably feel the breeze. But stirring up the air was about all his swing did, for the kid rarely made contact. He finished his swing with a dynamic, news-photo follow-through that seemed to please him more than anything else since being called up from the minor leagues.

I put his swing on videotape and asked him to look at it when we got back to the clubhouse. I ran it a couple of times and then once again in slow motion without saying anything. The kid sat there spellbound by his own image.

Finally I asked him, "What's that look like to you?"

"Well," he said, "it looks pretty *good!*"

"How?"

"Well, I *look* better that way. And it's gonna help me hit more home runs."

"No," I said, trying to let him down easy, "that's gonna cause you an awful lot of grief. Look, you're a .300 hitter. That's what your ability is, and you ought to be happy. You're never going to hit more than fourteen to sixteen home runs a season. But if you keep up like this, you'll ruin what you've already got."

He didn't take it what you'd call "well." But being the bearer of unpopular news is sometimes part of a coach's job. Another part is being patient and realizing that you're dealing with human egos. Hell, I've been there myself. Eventually, as his average began to drop, the two of us began to work on restoring his old form and he began to hit around .300 again.

But there are a lot of players who, let's face it, just aren't that smart. I don't mean they're necessarily dumb. I mean they let their egos outweigh their common sense. There are an awful lot of players at *all* levels who want to look like hitters they admire.

"If I don't look like so-and-so, I'm not going to change," they say, regardless of the poor results their imitations produce. In one or two extreme cases I've run into a .220 hitter and tried to talk a little common sense about where he should hold the bat and such, only to have him look at me and say, "Well, I don't look like the norm."

What on earth is the "norm," and what difference does it make *how* you look? Al Cowens used to hold the bat up by his eyes, since that was the spot from which he could most easily reach the launching position. People laughed like hell at him—until he was chosen the second most valuable player in the league.

I think part of the problem is that people see pictures in the sports section of the paper that mislead them. If it's a batter, for some reason the picture is always taken at the end of the follow-through. People see the player standing there, his legs out, his body twisted back and around—a perfect symbol of complete effort. Yet by the time the picture was taken, the swing's all done. You don't see the point of contact.

So understandably, I think, some people tend to concentrate on how they'll look in the follow-through. And before long, that newspaper picture burning in their brains, they're worried more about how they'll look when they finish the swing than whether or not they hit the ball in the process.

LOOKING FOR CONTACT VS. HOW YOU LOOK

This concern for appearances influences a batter in other ways as well. There are some guys, for example, who would rather take a big swing and hear the crowd go "Ooo" and "Ah" than make contact. They're so concerned about how they look—"Do I look like so-and-so? Do I have his style?" —that they forget what they're there for.

Big home-run pull hitters are especially vulnerable to this kind of vanity. I mean, you've got a man on second and a man on third. It's the twelfth inning, and there're two outs. A simple base hit and you win the game. Yet as the big left-handed pull hitter steps up to the plate, the entire opposing team shifts over to the right, opening up one whole side of the infield. If the guy wants to take the bat and just bunt the ball to one side of the infield, they give it to him.

But the opposing team knows that the hitter's mentality isn't enough or that his ego's so overgrown that he just won't hit a ground ball or a liner to win the game. He's got to look good. He's got to take a big swing and gamble on pulling the ball. Believe me, I've been there and I've seen it. And sometimes it just makes me sick.

The same thing happens in Little League or Pony League ball. How many times have you seen a kid come back from home plate after striking out with a big swing? He didn't watch the ball. He didn't put it into play. "Well, if you'da hit it, you'da really creamed it," his buddies say. But he didn't even make contact when a simple base hit could have driven in the winning run.

There are many times in the course of a game when all you're looking for is contact, times when as a coach you want to shout, "Just hit the ball, dummy, and you're gonna score a run." But no, the player wants to look good. He wants to take a big swing, even though that means trying for more than he's capable of or more than common sense dictates.

Even if you have the ability and are a successful pull hitter, the smart thing to do is to give in a little bit when you've got two strikes on you. Adjust your mentality and just try to hit the ball. Just put it into play. You may make out, but as long as you make hard contact, you've at least got a chance to advance any runners on base if you don't get on yourself. And that's a lot better than continuing to try to pull and striking out.

HITTING TO ALL FIELDS

To me that's just plain common sense, a quality that, as you can tell by now, I put a big value on. It's a commodity that's always in short supply in any field of endeavor (which makes you wonder why they call it "common"), and the baseball field is no exception.

Common sense is why I think players, especially young players, should try to hit line drives and let the home runs take care of themselves. This results in hitting to all fields, an Absolute that most great hitters followed most of the time. But that fact won't prevent home-run opponents from tagging you as a Ping-Pong artist.

Well, that's okay. I just remember times like when the Yankees played Texas a while back. Before the game I asked Oscar Gamble to go over the Rangers' batting order for me. Oscar's a d.h. (designated hitter) outfielder for us and a superb hitter. He came from the Rangers, and if you play on a club you get to know what your teammates can hit and what they can't.

So I asked Oscar how he'd pitch to Richie Zisk. He said, "If Zisk's swinging good, you can pitch him high and tight or low and away. But put it in the middle and look out." Then he went to Al Oliver. "Oliver's the best hitter they've got. He'll stand there and hit a line drive here and there and there," Oscar said, gesturing with his arm. Then he paused and said, "You know, *your* kind of hitter, Charley."

Nothing will ever change the fact that it's the line-drive hitter who's going to get on base most often. He's consistent. Day after day after day he's the guy who's going to hurt you.

And that only stands to reason, since the line drive is the hardest kind of ball to field. Sure, if a guy's standing in the right place at the right time he can reach out and snag it. But if you hit *enough* of them, you're going to be successful. You want to keep the ball out of the high-pop area and more in the chest area. That should be your goal. Let the mistake be the home run or the hard ground ball.

Look at it this way. Suppose you go up to the plate thinking and aiming at "right center" or "left center," depending upon the way you bat. Or suppose you just think of knocking the ball right back at the pitcher's forehead. Or whatever. The point is, you're thinking "middle" or "center."

If you've got a good swing using all the Absolutes and are the proper distance to and from the plate and the pitcher, you're going to hit and hit hard. You can aim at the middle of the field and still hit hard, long balls.

But every at-bat is different. You're dealing with two human beings and a whole set of constantly changing variables every time you step up to bat. Pitchers bring the ball at anywhere from forty to ninety miles per hour. Your reaction time and that of the guy on the mound aren't the same pitch after pitch or day after day. Sometimes the ball breaks or sinks or rises or does something else. In short, all *kinds* of things can happen to prevent you from hitting the ball to the center-field area, which is your target.

So you're not always going to achieve your goal. But look what happens as a result of simply *aiming* in that direction. If everything's perfect, you'll hit a line drive right back through the box (that is, through the "pitcher's box," a term held over from the 1800s, when pitchers stood in a rectangular area similar to the batter's box). If you're a little late, you'll hit it hard to the opposite field. If you're a little early, you'll pull the ball for a possible home run. So even if you make a "mistake" and don't manage to line the ball to center, you've still got a much better chance of getting on base than someone who tries to pull the ball. Pull hitters, remember, rarely make consistent contact when they don't hit for distance. It's an all-or-nothing proposition.

If you've got a good swing using all of the Absolutes, and if you try to hit a line drive to center field every time you come up, the percentages are in your favor. Do this enough times and you're going to hit your share of home runs and doubles. You will hit to *all* fields. And you'll be consistent.

This is why I can be so confident when I say that a player can raise his average thirty points and possibly hit more home runs if he will try 100 percent of the time to hit the ball back at the pitcher's forehead. Given a good swing, it's really that simple.

Here's the complete swing from its beginning preparatory movement to its completion in the follow-through. You'll want to examine each photo closely, noticing how it differs from the one before it as the swing progresses and how George Brett demonstrates the Absolutes of good hitting. But before looking at details, scan the entire sequence quickly. You'll find that seen as a whole the swing is powerful and intense yet at the same time graceful and fluid. This is the goal of every aspiring hitter, and George Brett demonstrates it superbly.

Now go back to examine the individual pictures. Photos 6-3 through 6-8 show the preparatory movement so essential to getting your rhythm going in the stance. In the first photo George has just completed his last practice swing. In

the next five shots he not only brings his bat back, but shifts his weight
back as well. Notice that this backward weight shift brings his front foot up
off the ground in photo 6-6. Also compare photo 6-3 with photo 6-8. You
can see that his weight has clearly moved to his back leg by the end of the
preparatory movement.

Photos 6-9 through 6-11 show you how to get into a well-balanced, workable
stance. The feet are just a little more than a shoulder's width apart. The bat is
held close to the launching position, and George's weight is forward so that
he's on his toes, and back so that most of it is borne by his firm, rigid back
leg.

And there's something else. These three photos shows a batter who is both
confident and aggressive. From the pitcher's point of view, this is definitely a
batter to be reckoned with. He's not afraid and looks perfectly capable of
hitting the best the pitcher has to offer.

Photos 6-12 through 6-18 show the stride. The rhythm has continued in the
stance, and in photo 6-12 George uses it to begin his forward weight shift. He
strides with his front toe closed, making a positive, aggressive motion back
at the pitcher. Again, this is obviously not someone you'd want to fool with if
you were a pitcher.

As the front foot touches down, in photos 6-17 and 6-18, the bat is in the
launching position. Notice how the forward weight shift causes the back foot
to begin coming up off the ground, and notice that the hips are still closed
at this point.

Photos 6-19 through 6-24 show the swing. The weight shift continues so that by
6-23, the weight is very close to being "on top" of the front leg. The back toe
is pointing at the ground. The front leg is rigid and firm, providing an excellent
foundation for hitting the ball.

The hips start to open in photo 6-19 as the bat begins to move. They continue
to open throughout the sequence, whipping around the remaining distance
just as the arms bring the bat to the ball. Notice the difference in the position of
the hips in photo 6-23, taken a split second before contact, and in photo
6-24, taken a split second after contact. The second picture shows the hips
completely open; consequently the left hip is just slightly closer to the
camera.

The hands lead the bat through as George swings "inside out." He gets complete
arm extension as he goes into the ball to make contact in front of the plate.
His head is down and his eyes are open throughout. He doesn't "come from
under" or uppercut (photo 6-23). He swings slightly down at the ball to get
on top of it and throws the bat head at the ball.

The follow-through begins in photo 6-25 and continues, ending with 6-32. George
hits through the ball with a weight shift so powerful that his back toe
momentarily comes up (photo 6-25). The momentum continues as the bat comes
around and the top hand comes off (photos 6-26 through 6-29). George doesn't
restrain it at all, letting the bat come all the way around (photo 6-30) so that
it nearly completes a circle by returning to a spot near its starting position. The
bat's momentum dies and George lowers it to the ground (photo 6-31).

Notice that George's head is down, exactly where it was at the point of contact,
even after he's well into the follow-through. Not until photo 6-30 does he
begin to move it. And even then, it's still pointed down at the end of the
follow-through (photo 6-31). That's great discipline of the head, requiring a lot
of practice and a high level of concentration. But, as you know by now, it's
one of the secrets of good hitting.

6-3

6-4

6-5

6-6

6-27

6-28

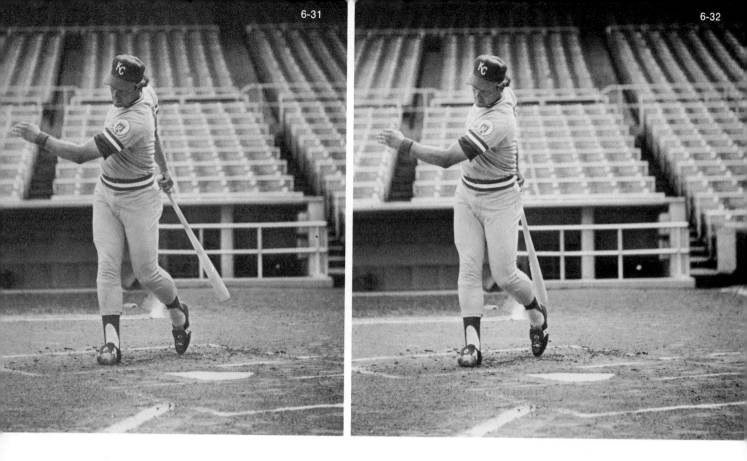

HITTER ANALYSIS

DALE MURPHY
HEIGHT: 6 feet, 5 inches
WEIGHT: 215 pounds
AVERAGE (1985): .300

For the past four years, Dale has hit 36 or more home runs each season, ranking him right up there with Mike Schmidt as one of the premier power hitters in the National League. In fact, 1985 proved to be one of his more productive years at the plate, with a .300 batting average, 37 home runs and 111 RBI. But Dale is more than just a home-run hitter, as he ranks second only to Hank Aaron in total hits for the Braves and is also a member of the exclusive 30-homer, 30-steal club.

This photograph shows Dale fully extended at almost precisely the moment he makes contact with the ball. Dale definitely has a balanced, workable stance. He also exhibits good rhythm and movement at the plate. This movement is in preparation for the swing and is necessary in order to relieve tension. Even the slightest movement can accomplish this, and Charley always felt that it was tension that could destroy a good fluid, graceful swing.

Dale also illustrates the perfect weight shift. He has that stiff front leg, and the toe of his back leg is sticking in the ground with his heel pointing up toward the sky. Like all good hitters, Dale has perfect balance at the moment of contact with the ball.

HITTER ANALYSIS

JOE DiMAGGIO
HEIGHT: 6 feet, 2 inches
WEIGHT: 193 pounds
AVERAGE (lifetime): .325

Joe DiMaggio was unquestionably one of the game's all-time greats, and here he is once again demonstrating the form that helped him compile such an impressive lifetime record. Although taken at an Old-Timers' Game when he was in his midfifties, the shot reveals a number of important characteristics of Joe's style. What stands out most clearly in this picture is one

Wide World

of the main things that comes to mind whenever I think of DiMaggio, and that is the sheer gracefulness of his swing. Tension-free; powerful but never strained or forced; Joe DiMaggio exemplified the smooth, fluid movement that is the ideal.

I'm not sure that this picture shows a really good swing. But it's a pretty fair demonstration of what you do to hit to the opposite field. Joe was obviously bent over at the point of contact. He didn't stand up to hit the ball. And he wasn't dominant with his top hand. Indeed, Joe has taken his top hand off here with all the thumb-to-forefinger elegance of a symphony conductor. Clearly Joe DiMaggio was a player who knew that power can be graceful and gracefulness, powerful, and that each is complemented by the other.

The Swing and the Follow-Through

HITTER ANALYSIS

REGGIE JACKSON
HEIGHT: 6 feet
WEIGHT: 195 pounds
AVERAGE (1985): .252

Few, if any, players in the big leagues are stronger than Reggie Jackson. And I'd say that tremendous strength is probably the most outstanding characteristic of his swing. It has allowed him to do things that other players would have trouble with and I think is the main reason for his success.

Sometimes, though, his strength works against him, making his swing less fluid and less fully extended than at other times. And sometimes he wants to swing too much with his top hand. Being so strong and being a left-handed hitter, this is probably to some extent unavoidable. I think it's caused some problems in the past, but recently Reggie's been able to channel it successfully. Whenever he hits to right center or left center, for example, the top hand has less of an effect, and he's more consistent.

I'd be less than honest if I didn't say that generally Reggie's mechanics have not been exceptionally good in years past. Yet his exceptional talent and strength have enabled him to be successful. Reggie's style works for him. But I'd hesitate to recommend it to anyone else, particularly to young players who may have the talent but not the strength to execute it successfully.

The Swing and the Follow-Through

7
OVERCOMING FEAR AND ELIMINATING TENSION

Know why the curve ball was invented? It was invented specifically to scare the bejesus out of the batter. The ball's change of velocity and its potential to deceive are important too. But they're really side benefits more than anything else. The main attraction is the fact that the curve ball appears to be headed right for the batter, only to veer away at the last moment.

This is also the main reason for switch hitting. Batters are scared to death of having the ball come at them and then go away. Whenever possible they try to bat so that the ball is coming into them.

Managers know this, of course. That's why you'll see them go out in the late innings to bring in a left-handed relief pitcher to throw against a left-handed hitter. It's true that, there being more right-handed pitchers in both leagues, left-handed batters aren't as accustomed to southpaw pitchers. But the real reason for making the change is that left-handed batters are generally very comfortable when the ball's coming from the other side. They're not nearly so positive when the ball's coming at them as it does when a left-hander is on the mound.

All batters, whether they admit it or not, are afraid of being hit by the ball. And the truth is, their concern is not without foundation. I'm worried for my hitters, for example, when someone with the speed of a Nolan Ryan is on the mound. Even the best pitchers make mistakes. The ball can slip or get misdirected. I'm worried because I know that if a batter is giving 100 percent, if he's doing his very best to get on base, and the ball slips, there's a good chance he'll get hit.

As a batter you sense this. You know that if he wants to, the pitcher can hit you. And it's the same on all clubs in both leagues. That's the advantage they have. They know they can throw the fear of the Lord into you if it suits their purposes, which is why you've got to admire someone who stands up there day after day and faces those hazards.

It's also why anyone who won't admit that the fear is real, that it exists, and that it touches them is a damn fool. Yet I sympathize with them. Even now it's a little tough for me to admit, but I was scared. Like many players, I used to try to disguise it. But the fear was there. It was real. And trying to hide it or ignore it didn't help. If anything, it made it worse.

You can't combat something you don't admit exists. And acknowledging that you're frightened is no reflection upon your manliness, your strength, your talent, or your courage. I remember once in the clubhouse after a game hearing Reggie Jackson say, "Damn, but I was scared tonight." I thought that was a great statement. Reggie has always had tremendous drive and courage. He knows that as a hitter fear comes with the territory and that pretending it doesn't exist is no way to handle it.

There's another guy I know of elsewhere who had the highest level of fear I've ever seen in a major-league ballplayer. He kept trying to disguise it or hide it, but it never did any good. Finally he came up to me one day and said, "Charley, you know I'm scared to death of that guy on the mound." I said, "Okay. Now we can try to find a way around this thing." And I think we did. But until this player admitted he was scared, he couldn't cope with his fear.

LEARNING TO ROLL

When you think about it, it's not at all surprising that a batter would be a little frightened, leaving aside the curve ball and any deliberate attempts by the pitcher to hit you. It's just not natural to want to stand there and put your head down close to where a bat and a ninety-mile-per-hour ball are going to collide.

I mean, I've been at practices where professional football players would come to work out with us. These were big, strong guys who'd gladly go out to butt heads with a locomotive. On the football field they could hit and be hit hard and not think much of it. But put a bat in their hands and throw them even easy pitches, and they were virtually helpless. Instinc-

tively, they'd back away from the plate. They'd do anything to get out of the path of the ball.

So there are a lot of good reasons to be afraid, but none that I can think of for not admitting the fact. And that really is the first step in coping with the problem.

The second step is to review your mechanics, particularly your balance. A young player who doesn't know anything about balance will tend to stand up straight and bend back away from the plate if he's frightened of a pitch. It feels safer to him than being bent forward, but it's the wrong thing to do.

It's not a natural reaction to lean automatically over home plate and thus toward the path of the ball. Either consciously or subconsciously, a lot of players want to be as far away from where the ball comes in as they can get. But there's a very good reason for bending forward at the waist, over and above the fact that it helps you hit the ball.

When you're bent over and in the proper stance, you're *balanced*. And as you know by now, that makes it possible for you to *move*—in this case, to move out of the way of the ball if necessary. It doesn't do much good to rear straight up since, with your feet planted and the top half of your body moving in that direction, you won't be able to go anywhere.

In the proper stance, your knees are slightly bent, your top half is leaning forward, and your eyes are on the ball. If you take your stride and the ball looks as though it's coming for you, you can easily turn your upper body back toward the catcher. This is called rolling, and it's something every player should learn to do almost by reflex. A roll is just a quick quarter turn with your upper body. You don't have to move your feet at all. It's the fastest, easiest, most effective way to protect your head and upper body. Rolling takes you out of harm's way, but if you do get hit, it lets you "take the punch" where it will cause the least trouble—on your front leg or on the tip of your shoulder, for instance. That's not fun, but it's a lot better than getting it in the head or the chest, which can happen if you rear straight up instead of rolling.

Of course, to be effective, this technique must be practiced, just as you practice other elements of hitting. I think that often the anxiety about getting hit makes you imagine that it's worse than it actually is. And in a way, you're kind of relieved once it happens. It hurts plenty, but you find that you can take it. Getting hit in the head is a different story, but batting helmets have been a big help in this regard.

One drill I've found to work especially well in developing a batter's ability to roll involves throwing tennis balls instead of baseballs. With a young batter, I'd start by standing relatively close and throwing easy. Then I'd back off and gradually throw harder. It's got to be a progression. When using this drill I throw strikes just as in batting practice, but every now and then I try to hit the batter. His job is to roll each time he sees the ball coming at him. Usually it doesn't take too long for this to become a reflex. And besides showing the batter how to protect himself, it also develops his confidence. Once he knows he can get out of the way of a pitch, he can be more positive and aggressive.

In a few very rare cases a batter will have what amounts to a sixth sense about the ball. It's almost a proximity sense, for these guys just seem to *know* where the ball is and where it's going to be. Two players who come to mind immediately are Ted Williams and Dick Stuart.

Both were successful hitters who'd go to the plate, get in there, and really bear down, yet I don't think a pitcher could hit either of them in the head. They'd sense the ball and simply move out of the way. (Of course, there are other guys a pitcher couldn't touch either, but that's generally because the guys don't get in there and try to hit.) Needless to say, most of us are better off learning how to roll.

OTHER FEARS

Anxiety about getting hit is the most serious of a batter's worries, but it's not the only fear he's got to deal with. There's also the fear of looking bad and the fear of losing his personal battle with the pitcher. I think these fears are probably more acute in the major leagues, where a man's professional pride is on the line. But the problem exists in one form or another at all levels.

No player, and in particular no major-league player, wants to get jammed on a fast ball, for example. By throwing the ball fast and in close, the pitcher hopes to jam the batter by preventing him from getting his arms extended in time. If the batter isn't careful, he either misses the pitch or hits the ball on the thin part of the bat, which often causes it to break. No player wants to break his bat under those circumstances, since a broken bat provides indisputable evidence that the guy goofed and let the pitcher jam him.

Nor does a batter ever want to let an inside pitch get by him. The ball inside is the one most batters can hit the hardest and the farthest. And if the pitcher succeeds in getting one of those babies by him, the batter feels he has failed. The pitcher has beaten him inside, and that hurts his ego.

Because they're afraid of looking bad, many players spend a lot of time training themselves to handle inside pitches, to be "strong inside." They won't go to get the outside pitch because they're afraid they'll look foolish or that the ball will get by them. This doesn't make a lot of sense, because the fact is that most successful pitchers pitch away, consistently putting the ball over the outside corner of the plate.

Professional pride and wanting to look good are fine. But when the fear of looking bad starts to interfere with a man's hitting—as it inevitably does—it's time to draw the line. No one gives a flying Frisbee how you *look*. As a batter at any level you're not there to win a beauty contest, you're there to hit the *ball*.

TENSION AND THE FEAR OF SUCCESS

If I were a psychiatrist I'm sure I could do a better job of explaining it, but there's another fear and it's the most puzzling of all—the fear of success. It can be a little hard to believe, but in baseball as in most other activities there are people who actually will themselves to fail. Maybe that's too strong. Maybe what they do is just will themselves not to succeed beyond a certain point.

They may not admit it and may not even be aware that they're doing it. But, for one reason or another, they don't try to the full extent of their abilities. The guy who's "comfortable" hitting .240 and refuses to do anything to improve his average may be an example of this.

I don't know, but I think maybe players like that are afraid of the pressure success might bring. After a good season they don't want someone saying, "Hey, if you hit .300 this year, there's no reason you can't do it *every* year." That puts them in the spotlight. And having demonstrated that they have the ability, they're afraid they won't be able to live up to that standard the following year. It's much easier and "safer" to avoid taking that chance and to stay where they are. Of course, I suppose they could just be lazy.

Still, this brings up an important point. And that is that success often does lead to pressure. But then so does failure. Whether he's trying to raise his average or just maintain it, a player is still under pressure to hit the ball. And in both cases, the pressure invariably leads to tension.

There's probably nothing that can destroy a batter's chances so quickly and so completely as tension. If you're tense, your body doesn't move smoothly. Your muscles get rigid, making it impossible to take the graceful, flowing, head-goes-down swing that is essential to hitting the ball. And your mind is distracted, making it impossible to concentrate.

WHERE TENSION COMES FROM

It often appears that there are *many* causes for tension. At the professional level, a player may have trouble at home. He may have just had an argument with his wife, or he may be worried about how his kids are doing or the bills he has to pay. A college or high school player may be just as worried about his grades, or a Little League player about impressing his parents. Or the player may just have goofed in the field, missing a throw or dropping a fly ball. His coaches and manager may just have yelled at him and, as he steps up to the plate, some fans may be yelling at him too. So he gets tense and he makes mistakes. He fails to get a hit, so the next time he comes up he's even more tense. He makes more mistakes and fails again. Pretty soon the thing's feeding upon itself, and he's sinking into a slump.

Surprisingly, though, the same thing can happen at the other end of the spectrum, with the guy who's really doing well. This is because the harder you hit the ball, the harder you *want* to hit it. If you play golf and happen to be swinging so well that you reach the green in two, or if you're on the tennis court and manage to really smoke one back at your opponent, the natural reaction is to think: "Well, damn, I can do that *all* the time."

The exact same thing happens in baseball. A hitter has a successful week. He's gotten twelve or fourteen hits and maybe three home runs. He's hot. So a sportswriter goes to him and says, "Hey, what happened? Why the success?" And the player says, "I'm seeing the ball." And he is. There's no tension. His head goes down as he executes a smooth, rhythmic swing and graceful follow-through.

But the only thing he remembers is the home run or base hit he pulled. He doesn't remember the ball he sliced down the opposite-field line or the three ground balls that went back through the middle. He remembers the home runs.

Now he says, "I can do this. I can hit home runs all the time." And all of a sudden he doesn't see the ball anymore. The tension comes back and begins to grow. And he no longer has success. Now he's got to start all over again.

What do the guy in the slump and the guy who's really hot have in common? They're both trying too hard. The player who walks out on the field desperately trying to hit the baseball is the player who's going to screw it up. Whether he's trying to bat his way out of a slump or keep a hitting streak going, the tension is the same. And although tension may appear to be the result of many different pressures, in the end it all boils down to the same thing: *trying too hard.*

It's an ironic fact of life that often what we try hardest for is the one thing we fail to achieve. It's almost as if the very act of trying for it pushes it out of our reach. And I think in many cases it's the tension that comes with trying too hard that's responsible.

I think that successful people in general—in business, in baseball, in all walks of life—are not tense. There's an air of confidence about them that comes from knowing what their ability is and doing their best to live up to it. In baseball as in everything else, it's the person who fools himself who gets into trouble. You've got to be honest with yourself and ask, "What is my ability? What am I capable of doing?" Then make a commitment always to do your best to play to the full limit of your ability.

When you try too hard, when you force yourself to attempt something that's beyond your ability, you inevitably get tense. And the tension causes you to fail, not only in trying to achieve your main goal but also in achieving anything else along the way. If you try to hit home runs, for example, and you don't have the ability to do so, you'll create so much inner tension that you'll not only fail to pull the ball, you also won't hit it at all. You'll simply strike out time after time.

This self-analysis cuts both ways, though. Being too soft on yourself is just as bad as striving for something you're not equipped to do. I don't agree with the .260 or .270 hitter who says, "Well, gee, I'm comfortable hitting this way." I don't think a player should ever be completely satisfied. And I know that playing to the full extent of your ability always take effort, so you can't be giving your all and still be "comfortable."

The ideal is somewhere in the middle. On the one hand, you don't want to be forcing yourself to do something you can't, but on the other hand, you don't want to accept less than your very best. Being honest with yourself about your ability and then always trying to live up to it is one of the best ways I know to ensure both maximum success and minimum tension.

And then there are the more exotic ways of controlling tension. I know one player, for example, who had such a high level of tension that he went to a certified hypnotist. After four or five sessions the mental wiring was complete. The player had what I think they call a posthypnotic suggestion. Every time he went to bat, he was supposed to touch his nose. This would switch on the mental machinery, and he would relax. At least that's how it was supposed to work. Whether it did or not, I can't say. I really haven't looked into that kind of thing. If it works, I suppose it's all right. In fact, in extreme cases it may even be necessary. But for most people I don't think I'd recommend it.

THE COACH'S ROLE

I think what most players need more is an understanding coach. I don't mean someone who's soft or who lets you get away with doing less than you're capable of. I mean someone who knows when a player needs to be praised and when he needs to be stepped on. Coaches have to be able to do both. But a lot of the time I think we do too much criticizing and not enough praising. In fact, knowing what I do about players, I almost think I'd rather err by praising them too much than by not doing it enough.

A little well-timed praise can help a player develop the confidence to get out of a slump. And it can help relieve the mind of a player who's worked hard to achieve a good average but is afraid he'll lose it. You see this a lot in the major leagues, where a guy's income and even his whole career can hinge on how well he does at the plate. But the same thing happens at other levels of the game, where the pressures may be different but just as intense.

A guy has worked hard for four months. He has a good year going for him, hitting .300 or better. But as the end of September approaches, he gets scared he'll lose it. It preys on his mind. "Here I've worked so hard. I've got it in my grasp. But I'm afraid it's going to slip away." If a player's not careful, simply worrying about losing his average will make him tense and cause him to do just that.

Exactly this kind of thing happened once when I was coaching at Oakland. Joe Rudi was having a great year. He was hitting around .305, but with about two weeks to go in the season he began to worry. Joe hadn't been swinging well, and one night as we were coming back on the plane he said, "Charley, I'm scared I'm going to lose it all."

"Joe," I said, "you're not going to lose anything." I thought back over the season and how Joe had worked to harness his tremendous ability. "You're going to hit .314 or .315. That's the way I feel."

And that *was* the way I felt. I knew he had the ability and the desire. I knew he could do it as long as he didn't get tense. Telling him as much just helped remove the burden he was sweating under. And as it turned out, he relaxed, kept his swing tension-free, and went on to hit .316.

THREE OUT OF TEN

So I think a coach's reassurance can be a big help to a player. But I also think it can help if a coach explains the numerical facts of life to his players. You know I've said that hitting a baseball consistently is the hardest thing to do in sports. And it is. But at the same time, if you define success as, say, a .300 average, you've got an awful lot of leeway to achieve it. A .300 average means that a player hits safely to get on base 30 percent of the time. That means he can make out seven times for every ten times at bat. He's only got to hit safely three times to be a success.

If you maintain a sound, common-sense approach to the problem, it's not all that hard to do. I think that if more players were made to see things from this perspective, they might not get so uptight about hitting for average. And without that tension, they'd have a much better chance at hitting .300 or better. Or if they aren't .300 hitters, of becoming winning hitters who perform to the maximum of their ability.

We've talked a lot about the mental aspects of eliminating tension. But there are certain physical things you can do that are equally important. This is one of the reasons why it's so critical to develop rhythm when you take your stance.

You can't be tense if you're moving. In addition to their other benefits, the practice swings you take, the bending at the waist and then softening the knees, and above all, the rhythmical shifting of weight that takes place in the proper stance all serve to eliminate tension. They keep you moving. They keep you loose.

As I've said before, these "one-two-three" mannerisms should become a habit. Your routine should be something you go through automatically, without having to think much about it. This is especially important where tension is concerned, for often you can be tense and not even know it.

For example, I'm not terribly proud of my golf game. I know I've got the ability to be much better than I am. So I work at it. And although I of all people should know better, I sometimes try too hard and I get tense. But the thing is, I don't *know* when that's happening. I'm not aware that there's anything wrong—until I swing and top the ball or see it slicing

into the rough. Then I know I'm too tense and I make a deliberate effort to relax.

A baseball player standing at the plate has the same problem. He can be tense and not know it until he hits or fails to hit the ball. But as a coach I can tell sooner than that, since I have the advantage of being an outside observer. Standing in the coach's box or dugout when we're at bat, I look at each player who steps up to the plate. If I see him moving in his stance, developing that crucial rhythm, I know he's got a chance. If he doesn't move, it's a pretty good indication that he's too tense and probably won't hit very well.

Generally, the players who have made movement and rhythm a habit are least bothered by tension. Whether they're aware of being uptight or not, there's no way tension's going to sneak into their swing. By making a habit of moving, they never give tension a chance to take hold.

Overcoming Fear and Eliminating Tension

8
DEALING WITH SLUMPS AND OTHER PROBLEMS

Anybody who's ever walked to home plate has been in a slump. Good players, bad players, mediocre players—from time to time they all experience periods during which they just can't seem to get a hit. For some, a slump may mean coming up to bat ten times without getting a hit. For others it may mean going zero for twenty or even zero for five. The definition depends upon the individual, his capabilities, and his past performances.

But regardless of definitions, the important thing to realize is that slumps are simply part of the game. Just because you're in one doesn't mean you've been singled out. Nor does it necessarily reflect on your ability or indicate that you're losing your touch.

TWO KINDS OF SLUMPS

Sometimes, though, it *does* mean that you're not paying attention to the Absolutes or to your mechanics. Earlier I mentioned the player on a winning streak who answers a writer's questions about his sudden success by saying,

"I'm seeing the ball." Well, all too often, when he's in a slump, that same player neglects to say, "I'm *not* seeing the ball." Yet that's often the cause of his problem. He just doesn't recognize it, for he probably doesn't realize how critical seeing the ball is to successful hitting.

Now, convinced that he can hit home runs, the player gets tense. He swings too hard. Maybe he overstrides. And he tries to pull. But regardless of its exact cause, the end result is nearly always the same: He no longer sees the ball the way he did when he was successful. Until he gets back to basics, back to the Absolutes, his slump will almost certainly continue.

Constantly striking out for lack of contact with the ball is one kind of slump. But there's another variety that can be even more damaging. And that's when a player hits the ball well time after time only to have it caught by the opposition. In a three-game series, for example, I've seen George Brett hit the ball hard twelve times out of fourteen at-bats and not get a single hit. I mean he hit *rockets*. But they were all caught or successfully defensed and he couldn't get on base.

That kind of thing is demoralizing. But George handled it well. A less mature player facing the same problem might easily have ended up developing the typical slump mentality. When a player's in a slump it isn't uncommon to see him moping around as if he were carrying the weight of the whole world on his back. He feels that everybody hates him. Nobody thinks he can hit, and before long he begins to doubt himself.

I like to compare what happens next to a bunch of guys playing poker. Suppose you're in a game and you're down five hundred dollars. Or let's make the stakes even higher. Let's say you've just thrown the deed to your house into the pot and have lost it. There's only an hour more to play and you want to win it back. Now you're struggling. Now you've got to push. Now you begin to grasp at straws. And as a result, you don't play very well.

If, on the other hand, you're playing and you've got the other guy's house, if you're ahead, you're going to relax. You're not going to draw to an inside straight or take foolish chances. You're going to sit back and play *good* poker.

The successful hitter, like the winning poker player, is relaxed. When he's hot and swinging good, he's usually swinging at strikes. He's patient. He waits for the good pitch and then connects. The guy in the slump, like the card player who's lost his house, gets panicky. All of a sudden the patience is gone. He swings at bad balls and gets himself out.

The man in the slump tends to grasp at straws. He gets tense and begins forcing his swing, which is the worst thing he could do. You can't force anything when you're trying to hit. You've got to wait for it to happen. Whether the slump is caused by a lack of contact or by the fact that the balls he hits well are caught, any player who lets a slump keep him from a cool, level-headed, common-sense approach to hitting is doomed to continued failure.

BEING ABLE TO COPE

A good player never lets himself develop a slump mentality, no matter how tempting wallowing in self-pity may be. For one thing, a good player knows his ability. He knows he can hit, and he's got the security and confidence that comes with past success. If he's not making contact, he takes the time to analyze his problem and makes corrections.

If the balls he hits well are being caught, he takes a more philosophical approach. Experienced hitters all know that these things run in cycles. Successful hitting is a matter of percentages. And if the percentages are for some reason against the player for several games, he does his best to not let it get to him. He knows that if he sticks with it and keeps hitting the ball well, those same percentages will eventually turn in his favor. Basically, the successful hitter knows that if he hits the ball hard enough, often enough, it all evens up over the course of a season.

It's part of being able to cope, and I saw a fine example of it in Reggie Jackson following a double-header with Detroit toward the end of the 1979 season. Reggie's dream was to hit .300 and that particular day his average stood at .297. He was so close he could taste it. But throughout both games he didn't get a hit. And his mechanics were very *good*. Reggie was a little puzzled, for like all good players he knows when he's functioning well. "How could I be so good and not get a hit?" he asked, but neither he nor I knew the answer. That's because there really *was* no answer. The cycle, the percentages, call them what you will, just weren't working in his favor that day.

Reggie handled it well. He didn't let it get to him. He kept at it. I doubt that most first- or second-year players would have the maturity to do the same. More than likely they'd be out walking the streets wondering what's wrong with them and starting to slide into the slump mentality.

WHEN YOU'RE YOUNG

I don't think there's any question that it's a little easier for the experienced, mature player to get out or avoid a slump. But I'm not so sure you can teach a younger player to cope. For one thing, the younger player doesn't have the security of past successes to see him through a bad period. He's not as confident that he really *can* hit. For another, he can't take the long view and look back over many past seasons to realize that slumps are just part of the game. You can tell him these things, of course, and he may nod in agreement. But without the actual experience his agreement may lack conviction.

Nevertheless, the coach's role when a player's in a slump can be crucial. There may be no substitute for experience, but by directing the player in the right way, a coach can help him through a slump and make sure that he learns as much as possible from it. As I look back I remember

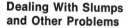

Dealing With Slumps and Other Problems

149

my dad doing so much to help me in that area. I'd go zero for three or whatever, and I'd really be down and my father would say, "Well, son, tomorrow's another day and the next game is another game."

As a player and a coach I've always tried to approach it this way. To hell with today. What's done is done, and worrying about it isn't going to solve any problems. Come out to practice tomorrow and we'll get to work on what went wrong. But right now forget it.

As a kid I remember going home with my dad after a game to get cleaned up and have dinner. Then later we'd sit and analyze each at-bat. "Did the pitcher get you out? Or did you get yourself out? Why did this happen? And what about that?" Whether I was swinging well or was in a slump we'd do this. My father believed in a cool, analytical approach and he believed a player should learn from his mistakes. I now have a lot more experience than my father ever had, and as far as I'm concerned, that's still sound advice.

GETTING OUT OF A SLUMP

Part of being a successful, well-rounded player is the ability to analyze what went wrong after you make a mistake. Whenever a really good hitter has struck out or grounded out or made some other mistake, he'll often come back to the dugout and say, almost to himself, "Damn, I swung at a bad ball," or "I should have *known* he'd give me that pitch," or "My weight shift was bad," or cite some other problem. With a good hitter, objective self-analysis of mistakes is almost second nature.

A coach can help a young boy develop that habit of mind, particularly when the player's in a slump. I also think that a coach can help make up for a young player's lack of experience and confidence by encouraging him to roll with the punches, to ride out the cycle. Some coaches, I know, yell at their boys and often take out their personal frustrations on them. And some parents of Little League players do the same thing whenever their kid makes a mistake. I think that's inexcusable. Hollering at a player, particularly at a young age, rarely does any good. In fact, I think it can only hurt him.

It's much better and more effective to say, "Look, you made a mistake. But there's no problem. Come out to practice tomorrow and we'll try to figure out what went wrong and how to correct it." Hard work and lots of practice are two of the best remedies I know for a slump.

Another is having the player hit the ball the other way—that is, have him avoid pulling, and have him hit to the opposite field. Or have him hit it through the middle, focusing on the pitcher's forehead. When a player sets out to do that, you know he's going to watch the ball, and you can be sure his mechanics will be pretty good.

Finally, when a player does well, I think a coach ought to tell him. Even if he makes out, if his mechanics were good, I think the coach should reinforce them: "You didn't get a hit, but you did good things up there. Just keep doing them and you'll be successful."

OTHER PROBLEMS

Over the years a whole catalog of words and phrases describing various hitting problems has been developed. You hear about "plate coverage," and "uppercutting," and "not waiting on the pitch," and so forth. I suppose these phrases are okay, but I can't help feeling that most of them are left over from a bygone era, an era that didn't have analytical tools like videotape and high-speed, high-resolution photography. It might be years before everyone becomes aware of it, but I think many of these terms and phrases may be out-of-date.

Some receive far more emphasis than they deserve. Some, like "keep your eye on the ball," are misleading because they aren't descriptive enough. And some, like "top hand" or "hit off your back leg," are misleading because they're simply incorrect. It's been my experience, though, that the fault they all have in common is that they focus on the wrong thing. They tend to treat the symptom instead of the disease, the effect rather than the cause.

As I say, I think a lot of these things were developed before very much was known about the swing. But now that modern technology has made it possible to study the swing in detail, I think you'll find that just about every one of the "symptoms" can be traced back to some failure in the batter's Absolutes. Consequently, the only sensible way to come at one of these specific problems is carefully to examine the batter's balance, rhythm, weight shift, and so forth. If, as a batter or as a coach, you're thinking along those lines, your orientation will be both different and more effective than the "traditional" approach.

UPPERCUTTING

Here's a good example of what I mean. Uppercutting is almost always caused by collapsing your rear leg before making contact with the ball. This lowers the rear half of your body and puts a big loop and uppercut in your swing. From that position you *have* to uppercut if you want to get the bat to the ball.

Now, you could concentrate on not uppercutting at the moment of contact and you could concentrate on not collapsing that rear leg. But you'd have better results if you focused on the Absolutes instead. Uppercutting can be caused or aggravated by a failure of several of the Absolutes. But let's take weight shift as an example. If you think: "I've got to get back to go forward, I've got to shift my weight forward and go to the ball," you'll be much better off than if you think specifically about avoiding an uppercut.

Here's one example of how it can work. If you're an uppercutter, you almost certainly have a very wide stance. Your feet are probably well beyond a shoulder's width apart. If you think "weight shift," you'll automatically bring your feet in, since the wider the stance, the harder it is to shift your weight. A somewhat narrower stance will make it easier to get to your front leg when you hit the ball, and that will make it both harder to uppercut and easier to hit the ball hard.

Would any of this have happened if you weren't thinking "weight shift"? Possibly, but I doubt it. You would have been focusing on your bat, trying to avoid an uppercut, and upon not collapsing your back leg prematurely. It probably never would have occurred to you to shorten up your stance or get to your front leg more effectively. You might have stumbled upon these things eventually, but think of the time wasted and the time spent practicing the wrong thing!

"YOU DON'T HAVE A LEVEL SWING"

Well, sure. Everybody's looking for a level swing. But the swing isn't always going to be level. And in searching for a level swing, the emphasis gets misplaced. Players concentrate on their arms and on the bat when the real question is: "How do we get there? What can we do so that the end result will be a level swing?"

These photos illustrate the lack of full extension that rolling your top hand can cause in some batters. Notice how the top hand forces the right elbow to bend (especially in photos 8-3 and 8-4), preventing full arm extension. Also, by photo 8-4, the top hand has caused the batter to throw his weight back on his heels, eliminating any weight shift he may have had.

Again, as with uppercutting, the answer lies in the Absolutes. Almost everything that happens *above* the waist is caused by what happens *below* the waist. If your base isn't fundamentally sound, the top half just won't work. Concentrating on the Absolutes will give you the firm base you need. If your weight shift is good, if you get to a firm front side to hit, a level swing follows naturally. In that position, it's much easier, for example, to swing level than it is to uppercut.

LACK OF FULL EXTENSION

This is a tension-related problem. It's caused by forcing yourself to pull the ball, by rolling the top hand over, and by trying to hit the ball too hard. Instead of thinking specifically about extension, you can solve this problem most effectively by focusing on your tension-reducing one-two-three mannerisms as you take your stance, on your rhythm and weight shift, on a tension-free swing, and on using the whole field to hit in instead of pulling.

POOR PLATE COVERAGE

As you know, I think "plate coverage" is one of those terms that gets more emphasis than it deserves. The place a player stands in relation to the plate depends a lot upon his body type. A guy with relatively short arms will

If this is your problem, you should stop rolling your top hand and consider taking it off the bat shortly after the moment of contact. Two hands on the bat at all times are fine, as long as they don't interfere with arm extension. But when they do, it's time to make a change.

naturally have to stand closer than someone with longer arms. But as I said earlier, I don't think there's a good rule of thumb about where to stand to ensure proper coverage. The main thing is to take some time when you're going into your preparatory stance. Set it up carefully and use a little common sense.

OVERSTRIDING

A player who overstrides usually begins with an exceptionally wide preparatory stance. I've seen some players who stand with their feet a yard or more apart. From that position the player either doesn't shift his weight at all or he has so much trouble getting back that it has little effect. In addition, a player who begins that wide usually ends up hitting with his weight "against" instead of "on" his front leg, and that robs him of a lot of power.

To cure the problem, you should return to the Absolutes. You think "weight shift" and "firm front side," instead of worrying about overstriding. Usually that causes you to automatically shorten your stance just enough to make the Absolutes possible, but not so much that you sacrifice aggressiveness.

HIT THE BALL WHERE IT'S PITCHED

I may be nitpicking, but I really don't care for this phrase. I think it's unclear and therefore misleading. What it means is if the ball's outside (away), don't try to pull it, hit it to the opposite field. If it's in the middle, hit it in the middle, back through the box. If it's inside, pull it.

I think the whole thing can be both simpler and clearer: "Use the whole field to hit in." Or, "Try to knock every ball right back at the pitcher's forehead."

NOT WAITING ON THE BALL

This is something else you hear every now and then, and I think it's just as unclear as telling someone to hit the ball where it's pitched. A player hearing the phrase for the first time is apt to think he should wait on the ball to get a better idea of what it's going to do. But that isn't what it means at all. The phrase refers to holding your reaction a split second longer so you'll have a better chance of hitting the pitch.

Every unsuccessful hitter in the big leagues has a quick hip. They react too soon or react by moving their whole body forward, and as a result they tend to step and swing at the same time. Stepping and swinging must be two distinct movements to hit well. The fine line between the two motions must be maintained.

Telling a player to wait on the ball gets him focusing on the wrong thing. It causes him to think about the ball instead of his mechanics. That's

why it's better to say: "Step first, then swing," or words to that effect. This way you get the player to concentrate on establishing a firm foundation before initiating the swing. You help him overcome a quick hip, and you accomplish the same thing as telling him to wait on the ball, with less misunderstanding and greater effectiveness.

9
BEATING THE PITCHER

It's a battle, plain and simple. When you're up there at the plate facing that other guy on the mound, you're in combat. He's going to use all of his wits and all of his skill to send you back to the bench as quickly as possible. And if you don't do the same—or you don't both outthink him and outplay him—you're going to lose. You'll be back on the bench so fast, your spot will still be warm.

I don't mean you've got to develop a personal animosity toward the pitcher in private life. I've known lots of pitchers and, off the field, they're generally not such a bad bunch. Besides, hating the pitcher can stir up emotions that can cloud your mind, make you tense, and hurt your performance.

Still, you should never forget the personal-combat aspect of a batter-pitcher confrontation and you should always think of the pitcher as the adversary, the man you've got to beat. A lot of batters have no trouble with this at all. But for some reason or another they don't take the next logical step. And that, to quote the U. S. Army and every military commentator since Julius Caesar, is simply "Know your enemy." In other words, take the time to assess the pitcher's natural ability. Pay attention to what he can and can't make the ball do. Then use that information to play upon his weaknesses and to anticipate the kind of pitches he'll give you in certain situations.

SIZING YOU UP

Knowing your enemy as a batter is particularly important because you can bet that the pitcher—if he's any good—has taken pains to know *you*. I could go to a Little League game, for example, watch a guy swing a couple of times, and tell where he can hit the ball best. I can tell whether he's strong inside or outside, whether he's especially vulnerable to an off-speed pitch, and so forth.

You've got to believe that pitchers can do the same thing. And, though perhaps not so much in Little League or at other amateur levels, they do. Here's how it usually works in the majors.

A new hitter—let's call him Big Joe Smith—gets brought up from Triple-A and he's very successful. Well, it takes a couple of months, but sooner or later the pitchers start talking about Joe Smith. Big Joe's just tearing everybody up and nobody knows how to handle him—yet. So the pitchers get together and start exchanging information: "How do *you* get him out? Well, how does John Doe do it? What's Big Joe do when he gets tense? How do we pitch this guy, anyway?" And before long they come up with a solution. They find his weaknesses, zero in on it, and just keep busting him there. Pretty soon Big Joe's not doing so well anymore.

Now, it's important to point out that this kind of thing is against league rules. It's called "fraternization" and a player can be fined a lot of money for engaging in it. But the fact that it's wrong doesn't always stop it from happening. After all, a major-league player usually plays with the same group of guys all through A, Double-A, and Triple-A. By the time he graduates to the majors, he's got friends all over the league. And then, too, players get traded from one club to another.

ANALYZING THEM

How it happens, though, isn't all that important. The point is that pitchers analyze batters. Pitchers try to avoid strengths and exploit weaknesses, and sooner or later the word gets around. Unfortunately, there are an awful lot of batters who fail to return the favor. Pitchers have strengths and weaknesses too, and these can be effectively neutralized or exploited by any batter willing to take the trouble to notice them.

When I was with Kansas City I remember going over the opposing team's pitchers with almost all of the Royals' hitters. We'd know whether a pitcher would let a guy pull or not, whether he had a good breaking ball,

change-up, or whatever. And we'd plan accordingly. Suppose, for example, we were facing a left-handed pitcher whom we knew couldn't execute away when pitching to a left-hand-hitting batter—that is, the pitcher's way of throwing, the rotation he put on the ball, caused it always to come back in to the left-handed hitter. In a case like that, the left-handers would go to the plate thinking "shortstop—over." In other words, they would deliberately avoid trying to hit the ball any place to the right of the shortstop. Instead, they'd concentrate on hitting it between the shortstop and the right-field foul line. If, on the other hand, the left-hander on the mound was able to execute away, the hitters would think "second base—over," which means hitting the ball from the second baseman over to the left-field line.

By doing this, the batters would step up to the plate already armed with the best strategy for defeating a particular pitcher. Based on prior knowledge of the "enemy" they could avoid his strengths and take advantage of his weaknesses. And they could do it from the very first pitch, with no wasted time or outs.

Paying this kind of attention to pitchers isn't anything new. From the beginning of baseball, batters have watched to see if a pitcher tips off certain things, to see if there are any mannerisms indicating that the next pitch would be a curve ball, a sinker, or whatever. And that kind of thing used to get around the league. It still does, of course.

But there's a lot more to analyzing a pitcher than knowing whether he telegraphs his pitches. Most major leaguers, in fact, are pretty good at disguising their throws. So you can't expect much in the way of a tip-off. What I'm talking about is the type of in-depth analysis that's practiced so infrequently anymore that it's in danger of becoming a lost art.

It used to be that all good hitters kept books or card files on what different pitchers threw and what they did in certain situations. Or maybe they kept it in their heads. But one way or another the information was there and ready to be used at any time. If a pitcher had a good curve ball, a good change-up, or a slider, they knew it. They knew whether he had a four-seam or a two-seam fast ball, or both. (Named for the number of seams crossed by the pitcher's fingers when gripped for throwing, a four-seam fast ball is thrown with full back spin and tends to rise as it comes in over the plate, while a two-seamer tends to go down or down and away.) And, since they had faced him before, they had a pretty good idea of what they'd see in most situations.

I've had pitchers tell me, for example, that they used to be scared to death whenever they faced Ted Williams because they figured he always knew what was coming. Well, Ted made a habit of analyzing the pitcher. He'd look for a certain pitch or for the ball to be in a certain location, depending upon the situation. And, most important, he had the discipline needed to make it work. If a home run can win the game, you look for a pitch you can hit for a homer. You don't swing at the first slider away or the fast ball. You wait. And if you've analyzed the pitcher you have at least some idea of when that home-run ball will appear.

Admittedly, it was easier to keep records years ago, since there were fewer teams in the leagues and you saw the same pitchers more often. Today you may not see some teams for two months. And it is true that most clubs have some form of pitcher analysis and records. But I don't think there's any real substitute for individual, personal notes (mental or otherwise) on opposing pitchers. And certainly there's no excuse for coming up to bat without even knowing the pitcher's name, something that's been known to happen even in the majors.

A NATION OF FAST-BALL HITTERS

In Little League and high school things are different, though. There the usual rule is: "Throw the fast ball until you get ahead. Then, once you're winning, throw the breaking ball." The reason is that at a lower level a pitcher usually has less control over his breaking ball. The fast ball is what he can throw for strikes, so that's what managers insist upon. Pitchers and managers everywhere hate a base on balls because they know a walk has a way of turning into a run. So rather than take a chance on a less than perfectly controlled breaking ball, the word goes out: "Fast ball! Fast ball!— Strike! Strike!"

To a lesser extent the same problem exists in the major leagues. There are pitchers who, from the day they're born, will never be able to throw the classic curve ball. In fact, there really haven't been many successful curve-ball pitchers at all. No one's ever been able to control it all that well day after day. So in order to compete, a lot of pitchers have had to find a substitute.

You hear of sliders, half curves, half sliders, little quick breaking balls, and so forth. But you can toss these terms out the window and just say "breaking ball," since in spite of the minute refinements, that's really all these pitches amount to. Most take years to develop, and all that time the guy's throwing mostly fast balls in games, at least until he gets ahead.

All of these fast balls have an important effect upon a hitter, particularly since he faces them when he's at a lower level and just beginning to develop as a player. In a word, they cause him to be *geared* for the fast ball. He expects it, and he's learned to hit it well since for so long fast balls are all he's had to practice on. Throw him a well-controlled breaking ball and you take him by surprise. He reacts too quickly to its slower speed, gets fooled by the way it comes in and breaks away, and ends up missing it or hitting it weakly.

This is what makes a good breaking ball such a damaging weapon. The fact that players don't expect it is at least as responsible for the breaking ball's effectiveness as the fear it creates and the way it fools the batter. But a breaking ball *can* be hit—if you're ready for it. In fact, if

lower-level pitchers threw as many breaking balls as fast balls, batters would adjust and we'd have a whole nation of breaking-ball hitters instead one filled with fast-ball hitters.

LOOK FOR THE PATTERN

But since that's not the case, a hitter's got to find his own solution. He's got to think about the pitcher, what the guy has thrown, what he *can* throw, and what he's likely to throw next. Keying on the individual pitcher is much more important than the rules of thumb you may have heard or how other individuals have pitched to you in the past.

I speak from experience. When I was a young player in the majors I used to follow blindly the 2–0/3–1 rule. Whenever the count was two balls and no strikes or three balls and one strike, I'd look for the fast ball. That's what they were *supposed* to throw in that situation, according to the rule of thumb. Only they didn't. They'd give me sliders or sinkers. They weren't very good pitches, but I'd swing anyway. And I'd miss. Eventually I woke up to what was happening and decided that I wasn't going to look for the fast ball anymore. I began to look for the slider or for the sinker.

I was a dumb hitter—until I realized that pitchers throw in *patterns*. It's the patterns that matter, not the rules of thumb. To some extent the pattern of each pitcher is different, depending upon the club he plays for, his own ability, the game situation, and so forth. Today, for example, whenever the Yankees play Detroit, I tell our hitters to watch out for the change-up. The Detroit team teaches its pitchers a change-up and puts special emphasis on it. So it only makes sense to look for that pitch, since in certain situations that's probably what you'll get.

You can do the same thing in Little League, high school, or college ball simply by watching the pitcher warm up. Can he get his breaking ball over? If he can, you can bet you're going to see it in the game. Does he have a slider? A sinker? A change of pace? Again, if he's got 'em, he'll use 'em.

That kind of information is essential. I mean an idiot can guess right 50 percent of the time and have some success if the guy's a two-pitch pitcher (fast ball and curve ball). But when you add the third pitch (the change-up) and the fourth pitch (the slider), the odds against guessing correctly are greatly multiplied. The more pitches a guy's got, the greater the need for intelligence and thoughtful anticipation on the part of the batter.

You can get the same information and a great deal more if you pay special attention to the pitcher the first time you face him in a game. Instead of forgetting about a pitch the moment it's in the catcher's glove, try to remember it. Compare it with the other pitches he gives you. Is there a pattern? Does he throw fast ball, curve ball, fast ball, or just fast balls? Can he keep his fast ball around your knees at the bottom of the strike zone, or does he let it drift upward toward your belt? What does he do when there're a man on first and two outs? What if there are none out? And so forth.

These are only a few of the questions you can and should be asking yourself when you're in the dugout or in the on-deck circle before going to home plate. And as the game goes on and you collect more information you can ask other questions. What did he do the last time? Is he cocky or getting tired? After a couple of innings you ought to be able to make a pretty good guess at the answers to these and other questions.

A BATTLE OF WITS

Part of beating the pitcher is knowing his capabilities and guessing what he will do. But another part is being aware of your own capabilities and faults. If you've got a weakness, you have to assume that the pitcher either knows about it already or will discover it very quickly. And you've got to assume that he will probably try to take advantage of it.

Of course, this doesn't always work. Roberto Clemente, for example, was a very smart hitter who went for years hitting around .350 or so. Since he hit the ball the other way (to the opposite field) so well, pitchers tended to avoid putting the ball close to the outside of the plate. That, they figured, would be playing right into his hands. Instead they kept banging him inside, figuring that the inside pitch was his weakness. It wasn't. Roberto actually *wanted* the ball inside. The ball low and away was the one that was toughest for him to hit.

So the pitchers guessed wrong. Or, more likely, at some point in his career Clemente recognized a weakness when trying to hit the ball away and made a real effort to correct it. That's a problem pitchers have when facing a good hitter. "Should I throw to his weak spot and just keep pounding him there? Or will the guy adjust and eliminate a weak spot that could be very useful sometime when I really have to get him out? Or maybe the batter knows about his weakness and will be *expecting* me to pitch there and I should therefore put the ball someplace else."

As you can see, this battle of wits between the pitcher and batter can get very complicated. Laced with uncertainty, second guessing, and incomplete information; heated by the emotions and tensions of the game; and executed by two fallible human beings, each with differing skills and abilities; it's enough to keep a Pentagon strategist awake nights trying to figure it all out. Yet the whole thing can be greatly simplified by a single fact. And that is that good hitters don't *have* big weaknesses. They may be able to handle some balls better than others, but the differences aren't significant. They detect any major weaknesses early and work to eliminate them as soon as possible. That's one of the things that make them good.

Another is instinct. All good hitters—in fact, all good players—have good instinct. And it shows. A good base runner, for example, is always noticeable. He hardly needs coaches to run the bases, for he seems to *know* when to run, when he can make it, and where the ball is. By the same token, a good hitter can often sense whether a pitch will be a ball or a strike, a curve or a fast ball, where the ball is, and where it will be when he brings his bat through.

Yet while good instinct is easy to see in a player and is frequently a criterion on scouting reports, it's not easy to define. As far as a hitter's concerned, it's something more than judging a ball by the way the pitcher holds or releases it. It's almost a sixth sense. Or maybe it's just that his brain has the ability to collect and synthesize hundreds of bits of information subconsciously and hand him a conclusion: "He's going to give me a breaking ball," or "This one will be a change of pace."

Whatever it is and however you define it, good instinct is one of those things you've got to be born with. I think everyone has some, and what you've got can be polished. But most of the great hitters, I think, had a lot to start with.

HITTING ANY KIND OF PITCH

Up to this point we've been talking about the mental part of the pitcher-batter battle. Now let's take a look at the other half—the physical part. Anticipating what the next pitch will be can help you decide whether to swing or not, and it can help your body prepare for the minute adjustments necessary to put the bat head on target during the swing. But you won't be able to make any *deliberate* mechanical adjustments. There simply isn't enough time.

A fast ball traveling at eighty-five miles per hour covers the sixty feet, six inches separating the mound and the plate in just under half a second. Even with the electrical impulse in your brain moving at the speed of light, that isn't nearly enough time to get your body to adjust for a fast ball, curve ball, knuckle ball, or whatever.

Batters who, because of the game situation, either have to pull the ball or hit it to the opposite field may move closer to or farther away from the plate. But that's not the same as trying to adjust to an incoming pitch. The only solution is to get into that groove where your mechanics are good and your swing is graceful and smooth. If your mechanics are good, if you follow the Absolutes, you have a chance to hit any kind of pitch.

What's more, your capability will show. A pitcher can sense whether or not you can handle his pitches strictly by how you look when you're at the plate. If he sees that you're balanced, that you don't have a quick hip, and that with each swing you're clearly aiming to shoot one right back at him, he's really going to be upset. Seen from the front, from the pitcher's viewpoint, a batter who had good mechanics looks dangerous. And I don't care how big or small you are, if your mechanics are good you can scare him to death.

A GOOD ZONE

Even with good mechanics, though, I don't believe you can handle all pitches at all times. I'm not even sure you can hit every pitch that's in the strike zone. I mean, just look at the variables. Among other things, a ball can come in high and tight, low and away, as an eighty-five-mile-per-hour fast ball, as a seventy-eight-mile-per-hour change-up, or as a curve ball that breaks three feet more or less. And that doesn't even take into consideration whether the ball's in the strike zone or not.

This is important, to say the least. How many hitters get themselves out by swinging at balls that are outside the strike zone? A lot more than most people realize. Most hits are made on strikes, pitches that would have been in the strike zone and would have counted as strikes if the batter hadn't swung. But if you take the .300 hitter—a player who fails seventy out of every hundred at-bats—you'd find that more than half of his seventy outs were made on pitches that were outside of the zone. For hitters with lower averages, the number is even greater.

If a guy has a good strike zone, he has it. Like good instinct, strike-zone awareness is something that's inborn. It can be polished and developed through practice, of course, but there's nothing like being born with it.

A FOOLPROOF WAY TO BEAT HIM

Yet while it's helpful to be born with good instinct or a good strike zone and while these and other gifts may make you a *great* hitter, not having them can't stop you from becoming a good hitter *if* your mechanics are good; *if* you make a habit of analyzing the pitcher; and *if* you will do one other thing. And that is simply to *gear yourself to hit the ball away and let the inside pitches take care of themselves.*

Of course, if the pitcher is pitching you in all the time, it's foolish to expect the ball to be away, and this general rule of thumb doesn't apply. But that's a relatively unusual situation. Something on the order of 94 percent of all successful pitchers in the big leagues pitch *away*. Yet only a somewhat smaller percentage of big-league batters gear themselves to hit the ball *inside*. It's incredible. It's crazy. But it's true.

Batters try to be strong inside for at least two reasons. First of all, there's the fear factor. A batter who's always opening his hip as he must to hit the ball inside is always getting out of the way. He's leaving the line of fire. The last thing he wants to do is to go get the ball outside, since that would mean sticking his nose over the plate and close to the ball. Second, the ball inside is the one the batter can hit for a home run, so he concentrates on it to the detriment of everything else.

Pitchers, on the other hand, pitch away in order to eliminate the home run. Part of the philosophy of pitching is: "Stay away! Stay away! Don't put the ball inside, where the batter has a chance to pull it." Realizing that everyone's trying to pull, the pitcher often plays on the batter's ego, tempting him to go for a pitch that is still away, but maybe not so much away as most. When the batter goes for it, he either misses it or hits it weakly, since he's not geared to hit that kind of pitch.

You show me a guy who's strong inside, a guy who can hit the ball from the middle of the plate in, and I'll show you a guy who can't hit when the ball's away (from the middle of the plate out).

But the same thing is *not* true in reverse. A player who's strong outside or away can *also* handle the ball inside. What's more, he can pull the ball when he wants to, and, because his mechanics are good and he's used to watching the ball, he can pull it *better* than someone geared for the inside pitch alone. In other words, if you work from the outside of the plate in, if you gear yourself to hit the ball away, you've got two capabilities going for you instead of just one. You'll be able to hit both the ball away and the ball inside, and you'll hit them well. That makes a lot more sense than being strong inside and thus writing off everything from the middle of the plate out.

Working from the outside of the plate in makes good sense for another reason. It lets you set the pitcher up and put him on the defensive. Here the mental and physical aspects of the battle merge, for by learning to hit the outside ball you show him that you can hit what he makes a living throwing. You sting him out there a couple of times and he's got to come in. He's got no place else to go. All of a sudden you've got him pitching to *you* instead of you trying to hit whatever he chooses to throw.

That in itself is something of a triumph, but it has other benefits as well. First and most obviously, it makes it possible for you to pull if you have to. And second, it frequently results in a slower pitch, even if the guy's throwing a fast ball.

Bringing the ball in more toward the center of the plate and closer to the batter is not an easy thing for a pitcher to do. There's a natural desire to avoid hitting the batter with the ball. Even though some pitchers do it, most have a hard time deliberately hitting a guy. Consequently, when they pitch inside, they're more cautious. They aim the ball more carefully and that forces them to sacrifice some speed.

Maturer, more experienced pitchers have learned to throw the ball hard to a given spot, so this doesn't affect them as much. But a lot of pitchers haven't developed that skill. So they take a little extra care, which takes a little speed off the pitch, which makes the ball *easier to hit.*

As I mentioned earlier, at times you may find a pitcher who keeps throwing you in. And in cases like that the general rule of thumb doesn't apply. It doesn't make sense to wait for the ball away in such situations because you're never going to see it. Usually the guy keeps busting you inside because he knows you can hit his pitch when it's away. So you've still dictated to him where he has to throw the ball. Often by just backing up off the plate a little you put yourself in position to hit his inside pitch as well.

BRAIN AND BODY

As you can see, beating the pitcher requires intelligent use of your mind and your body. You can bet the pitcher's using both his brain and his arm to beat you, so if you expect to win, you can do no less yourself. Good analysis and good mechanics make a nearly unbeatable combination. In fact, in the long run, over the course of a career or a season, I think the combination may well *be* unbeatable. Good analysis gives you a better idea of what's coming, and good mechanics give you a better chance to hit it once it arrives.

HITTER ANALYSIS

HAL McRAE
HEIGHT: 5 feet, 11 inches
WEIGHT: 180 pounds
AVERAGE (1985): .259

Hal McRae, seen here stroking a two-run homer in the '77 American League playoffs, is what's known in baseball as a "tough out." A tough out is a guy whose maturity and mastery of hitting have brought him to the point where he simply has no major weaknesses. You can pitch him in, out, or right up the middle, and he'll still hit the ball. Hal's the last guy an opposing pitcher wants to see at home plate when there are two out and a man on third, since Hal will score that man with greater frequency than almost any other player in the major leagues.

A close personal friend, Hal McRae is also one of the players most dedicated to winning in all of baseball. His determination at the plate is unsurpassed. Though perhaps not blessed with the same natural ability found in a lot of other people, that fact has never stopped him from developing a sustained, pitch-after-pitch concentration that's almost awesome to see.

But it wasn't always that way. Hal came to Kansas City from Cincinnati, where he had been a part-time player and a very successful pinch-hitter. As a pinch-hitter in the National League, he could usually count on getting a fast ball to hit somewhere. So he spread out his stance, got closer to the plate, and swung hard, all of which you can do with a fast ball, if you know how.

However, when he went to Kansas City this habit immediately

caused him some serious problems. Although it's gradually changing, I think there might be a little difference in the philosophy of pitching between the two leagues. Very few National League relievers, for example, would throw you four breaking balls in a row. Somewhere along the way you could almost count on getting a fast ball. That's what Hal used to look for, and when he saw it, he'd send it.

The American League, however, has always been more of a breaking-ball league. When the count's 2–0 or 3–1, you probably won't get the fast ball you could expect in the National League. You'll get a slider or a curve, even if it's the fourth breaking ball in a row. So when McRae went to the American League with his fast-ball-oriented style, he found he couldn't cope.

He had to change, and he had to accept the fact that he couldn't concentrate on hitting home runs and still be as successful as he wanted to be. So, like Lou Piniella, he began to focus on just hitting the ball. Hal is one of the most dedicated, hard-working players I've ever known, and before long he began to have success.

An intelligent, analytical player, McRae is very good at knowing what the guy on the mound can and can't do and at figuring out how to use his own talents most effectively against any given pitcher. In fact, I don't think I've ever seen another player battle the pitcher so hard and so relentlessly, which is one of the reasons why Hal McRae beats the pitcher so often.

Wide World

HITTER ANALYSIS

CARLTON FISK
HEIGHT: 6 feet, 2 inches
WEIGHT: 215 pounds
AVERAGE (1985): .238

Although Carlton did not hit for a high average in 1985, he did have his best power year ever, hitting 37 home runs and knocking in 107 runs. In part this was due to a weight and strength program he participated in during the off-season.

Carlton became a strong advocate of Charley's style of hitting when he joined the White Sox as a free agent just prior to spring training in 1981. At this time, Carlton got into the habit of practicing Charley's hitting routine. During training, players would use the entire field to hit in. For Carlton this meant hitting to the right side, getting full extension on all his swings as he backed off the plate, and having his weight going from back to forward in a more pronounced way.

Carlton moves around a good deal at the plate for better balance and rhythm in his swing. He also demonstrates good weight shift as well as an ability to keep his head down.

One of the most important things he learned from Charley was to get better extension by releasing his top hand after the swing. This is probably a good reason why his home-run production shot up so dramatically in 1985.

This photograph shows Carlton moving into the ball just as he's put his foot down. It is a great shot, depicting his amazing power of concentration, as it shows his head going down. You can actually see the tremendous weight shift, his back foot driving forward against the front leg. Again, this shows the positive, aggressive motion back toward the pitcher; at the same time it illustrates that good weight shift from the firm rigid back side to hit from a firm rigid front side.

Though not reaching his career average of .275, Carlton showed in 1985, at age thirty-seven, that he still possesses enough power to hit the ball out of the park, as well as an ability to come through with the timely hit.

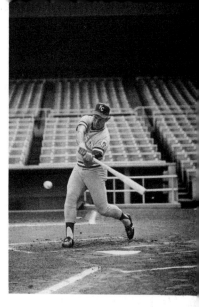

HITTER ANALYSIS

ROBERTO CLEMENTE
HEIGHT: 5 feet, 11 inches
WEIGHT: 175 pounds
AVERAGE (lifetime): .317

Roberto Clemente was a superb athlete, and for a period of four to eight years I think he may have been the most complete player in baseball. A lifetime average of .317, a four-time league batting champ, a twelve-time All-Star, twelve Golden Glove Awards, 1966 National League Most Valuable Player . . . the stats go on and on.

Here you see him swinging against Jon Matlack on September 30, 1972. This swing resulted in his three-thousandth hit, a double to center field and the last hit of his career. This is kind of unfortunate, since looking at it now, it's obvious that it's not going to be a good swing. I think he's been fooled by the ball. I think he was probably looking inside and the ball turned out to be away. Consequently he's not well balanced and is squatting down a little. I think he may have tried to check this swing but was unable to stop it. Nevertheless, it's a tribute to his great body control that he still hit it the way he did.

It's the kind of control you often find with great athletes, men who are able to combine strength with flexibility to create a smooth, graceful motion. I think you find that players of Clemente's caliber also tend to use good mechanics almost naturally, without really having to think too much about them.

Clemente, for example, stood off the plate, yet he still coped effectively with the ball outside. He had excellent arm extension, and, in fact, was one of the first players I noticed taking his top hand off the bat.

Nor did Clemente try to pull the ball. In fact, I think he made a conscious effort to hit the ball the other way. He counted a double to right center the same as one down the right-field line, and I think he was very proud of the fact that he could do both.

I don't know why it would be, but I've noticed that a lot of Latin players—Orlando Cepeda, Rico Carty, and the Alou brothers come to mind immediately—have this same philosophy. And, as with Clemente, I think it's an important factor in their success. All good hitters use the whole field to hit in.

HITTER ANALYSIS

FRANK ROBINSON
HEIGHT: 6 feet, 1 inch
WEIGHT: 183 pounds
AVERAGE (lifetime): .294

Frank Robinson was a great hitter for a long period of time. And longevity, as well as consistency, are things you've got to have to be considered one of the game's greats. Frank was also very strong. In fact, until I met Reggie Jackson, Frank Robinson had the strongest upper body of any player I'd seen.

Originally Frank held his bat nearly flat in his stance. The handle rested on his top hand like a lever on a fulcrum, and the bat head actually pointed down at the ground. Later he went to the opposite extreme and held his bat very nearly vertical. Like Henry Aaron, Ernie Banks, and Boog Powell, Frank Robinson also took a hitch down when he swung.

But that isn't what really stands out in my mind about him. Frank was one of the most fearless players in baseball and one of the very few I've seen who were successful crowding the plate. It's not all that obvious from this picture, but Frank was always on the plate in his stance. The only place you could pitch him was high and tight. He had to react very quickly, but his mental toughness allowed him to do it.

The mistake a lot of pitchers made with Robinson is the one pitchers frequently make with batters who crowd the plate. They try to put the ball over the outside corner and keep nipping there to get the guy to swing. But eventually they make a mistake and the ball ends up over the plate. That's the pitch a batter like Robinson will always cash in on.

The other alternative from the pitcher's point of view is to go inside. And if the pitcher has a good fast ball that comes into the batter instead of away (where it might end up over the plate), that's probably the route he should take. It's a question of where he executes better. Does he make more mistakes trying to nip outside or coming in?

The thing to be aware of as a batter is that this is the way a good pitcher thinks. This is how he analyzes you and decides how to pitch you. Another thing that some pitchers will do with a guy like Robinson, for example, is to pitch him bad inside the first couple of times and then go away from him the rest of the night. The idea is to establish "inside" before you go away.

And often it works. As a hitter, if somebody keeps throwing me inside, inside, inside, it tells me that I have to react a little faster and open a little quicker to hit the ball, particularly if I'm on the plate like Frank. Now I've got "inside" on my mind, and all of a sudden the pitcher goes away. But here I am reacting with the extra speed needed to hit the inside pitch. I've prepared myself mentally to hit exactly the opposite of what the pitcher is now giving me.

Frank Robinson was usually able to cope with this situation. But I've seen the technique destroy the timing of younger, less experienced, and possibly less talented batters. This might not have happened if they'd had a better idea of what they were up against and had been thinking more about beating the pitcher.

10
PRACTICE: THE KEY TO STAYING SHARP

t to all fields? How do you learn to shift your weight,
ake the "perfect" swing? There's one and only one
ice, practice. There's just no substitute. You've got
hit, and then hit some more.

only way there is to transform the Absolutes into
ou'll do without thinking when you're under the
in a game. When the Absolutes become a habit,
ur body to use good mechanics, your mind can be
her or focus on the game situation. You don't have
ut whether you're getting back to go forward,
to the launching position, and so forth. If you've
your body and your bat will be right where they're
supposed to be when they're supposed to be there.

Good hitters have good work habits. They know that practice and
lots of it is the surest way to eliminate slumps. And they know that practice
is essential to maintaining their edge. Consequently, good hitters are usually always working on something.

Hitting a baseball consistently is such a complex task that it isn't likely a player will ever reach perfection, at least not for very long. Out of a hundred swings, even the best hitters can expect perhaps only five that could be called "perfect." The other ninety-five may be damned close, but there are just too many variables to make perfection possible more frequently than about 5 percent of the time. In fact, I think you'll find that the minute you're sure you've got it all figured out, it'll jump up and bite you. You'll just always be working on something.

Major-league teams realize this, though some are more aware of it than others. As a result there are a number of good-hitting ball clubs whose rigorous practice schedules have produced a lot of disciplined, hard-hitting batters. But that kind of practice or even the somewhat less demanding workouts of other teams is the kind of thing the fan rarely sees.

There's spring training, of course. And there's practice during the season. Whenever the Yankees are on the road, for example, we hit early. I'll pick two or three guys for what we call "extra, extra hitting," and we'll go out early in the afternoon before regular batting practice starts. I'm especially interested in getting out there the guys who aren't playing every day, to help them stay sharp. But sometimes one of the regular players will be having trouble and we'll get together to see if we can adjust something to eliminate the problem.

The fan doesn't see this kind of intensive practice. And, while some come out to watch batting practice a couple of hours before a game, most people don't even see that. As a result, I think a lot of lower-level or amateur players aren't aware of how much major leaguers practice and of how important it is to them.

LIMITED RESOURCES

If practice is important to a professional ballplayer, it's even more important to a Little League or high school or college player. But here you run smack into the problem of limited resources. In the big leagues it's not uncommon to open a fresh case of baseballs whenever batting practice is held. Nor are bats broken during practice a concern. We've got a room full of new bats all ready to go. But then these are the tools of our trade. It would hardly make sense to hire ballplayers and coaches and not supply them with what they need to do their jobs.

At the lower levels, though, equipment can be a problem. Bats and balls cost money and usually there's never enough to buy all the things a team would like. Limited time is also a problem, particularly where coaches are concerned. Many coaches at the lower levels are either volunteers who work long hours because of their love for baseball and their desire to help young boys learn the game, or they're men who accept only enough money to cover their expenses. And, of course, some are professionals. But whatever the case, very few of them have the time to

work exclusively on hitting. They've got a whole team to worry about and many other skills to help players develop.

The fact that the coach's time is limited has at least two implications for players who want to work on their hitting. First, it means that young batters often don't get the advice, criticism, or praise they need. Without the coach there's no one to give the batter the vital feedback that can come only from an outside observer. You may *think* you're shifting your weight properly, for example, but without input from someone who has watched your swing, you probably can't know for sure. Or if you are shifting your weight, maybe you're not shifting it enough. Even at the major-league level players need the kind of feedback only a coach can give.

The second problem is even more troublesome. And that is that most lower-level pitchers aren't very good. A lot of them can pitch for an hour and in that time throw only five strikes. It's understandable. After all, they're young and trying to develop their skills just as you are. But it doesn't change the fact that batters *need* to swing at strikes, and the scarcity of well-pitched baseballs at the lower levels makes it extremely difficult for a player to get the repetition that's so vital to developing a big-league hitter.

Ideally, I suppose every amateur team should have a pitching machine. The machine could be set to deliver nothing but strikes, and that would solve the problem. But such machines are expensive and well beyond the range of most Little League or school treasuries. The next best solution is to have the coach do the pitching, since most coaches can throw strikes more often than their young players. But as I've already said, the coach's time is frequently quite limited.

WORKING ON YOUR OWN

So what can you do? The best answer, it seems to me, is to supplement your team practice with a lot of work on your own. A couple of guys with a bat, a backstop, and a bunch of baseballs can accomplish an awful lot if they want to improve and are willing to work at it regularly. You'd be surprised at how much it can help.

When I was growing up, my cousin and I lived next door to each other. There was a chain-link fence bordering our backyards that separated them from the schoolyard on the other side. We both worked but we spent what spare time we had practicing our hitting. And we took advantage of that fence.

We scrounged around and found some chicken wire and scrap wood, which we used to add about ten feet of height to the fence. The fence was six feet high to begin with, so when we were finished we had a hitting area about thirty feet long and sixteen feet high.

We used a basketball backboard as a backstop. And since my dad

Practice: The Key to Staying Sharp

was the manager of the town team, we had a couple of bats and maybe a dozen balls to work with.

My cousin and I would throw to each other, which, incidentally, improved our arms. But it was hitting that we were really interested in. The rules were simple. The guy at bat was allowed to hit as long as he kept the balls on our side of the fence. Once they had all been knocked over, we'd climb the fence, collect the balls, and exchange places when we got back.

It was hard work, but it was something we enjoyed doing, and the competition between us kept things interesting. And we kept improving. At first it was a big deal to be able to hit one line drive after another and keep all the balls on our side of the fence. Then, as we became even more proficient, we found we had to put a screen up in front of the guy who was pitching to keep him from getting hit so often.

Obviously practicing like this didn't cost the coach any time, and it certainly didn't cost a lot of money. Even if we'd had to buy the chicken wire, the bats, and the balls, the investment wouldn't have been too great, not when you consider how much we used them and what we got out of the experience.

It was through these hours and hours of practice that I learned to handle a bat and developed a good swing. And, of course, my cousin improved his skills too. Both of us, in fact, were invited to play pro ball, and both of us signed bonus contracts. I can look back and it's clear to me that the single most important factor in my becoming a professional baseball player was all that practice. Without it I'd never have become a decent hitter and never would have made it to the big leagues.

PLAYING PEPPER

Another good way to work on your swing that doesn't require a coach's presence or a lot of equipment is a pepper game. This drill's probably as old as baseball itself, and all it takes is a batter and a couple of fielders. The fielders stand in relatively close to the batter and take turns tossing him the ball. The batter hits it back at them at less than full force. The batter usually exchanges places with one of the fielders after a while so everybody gets a good workout. When played as briskly as it should be played, a batter can get in a lot of swings and work on developing a smooth stroke.

Unfortunately, a pepper game can be a little tough to get going when the players are very young. Usually they're just learning baseball skills and can neither catch, hit, nor throw the ball very well. But even at a young age, there are a lot of things a player can do to work on his hitting.

One thing you can do, for instance, is simply stand with a bat in your hand and practice your stance and swing. In fact, I'll make it stronger than that. This is something you *must* do to get accustomed to good mechanics. Even if you've been playing only a short time, you've probably already got some bat habits that have to be overcome. Old habits can seem very comfortable, and depending upon the individual, it can take a while before the Absolutes feel as good. That's why it's important to practice just your stance and your swing at first, without the distraction of trying to hit the ball.

LEARNING TO ANALYZE A SWING

The action photos in this book can be a big help. I'm not saying you should try to duplicate George Brett's swing, but I do think you should use the pictures as a guideline. Make whatever modifications are necessary because of your own body type or because of what works best for you. Just be sure that you incorporate all of the Absolutes, even if they're slightly modified to suit you.

I'd also suggest studying these pictures with a friend. Try to develop an awareness of the specific points I've talked about in this book and of how they look when executed by a batter. It will take some time, but if you stick with it, you'll find one day that you're seeing hitters in an entirely different way. You'll be able to tell whether a guy is back or not, whether his bat position is workable, whether he's seeing the ball or not, and so on.

As you're learning, watch ball games on TV and zero in on the batter. Pay special attention to his stance, his timing, his swing. Does he have rhythm and movement in his stance or does he stand rock still? Does he stride and then swing or run the two motions together? Does he have a quick hip? Does his head go down when he swings? Does he get a hit in spite of not following the Absolutes, and if he does, what does his batting average say about his consistency?

Asking yourself questions like these and maybe discussing them with a friend can make a televised ball game both more entertaining and enormously instructive. But I ought to add a word of caution.

Everything happens so fast in a swing that you will have trouble seeing everything at once. Don't let that frustrate you. Instead, concentrate on watching for only one or two Absolutes at a time. For one inning or perhaps until each player has been up one time, you could focus on stance and bat position. Then for another period of time, concentrate on swing or follow-through or top hand or something else. Also, the slow-motion replays are a great help.

Eventually you and your friend or friends will get to the point where you can analyze each other's stance and swing. You'll know what to look for and will be able to spot each other's deficiencies. That can ease the burden on the coach and make the time you spend practicing on your own much more productive than it otherwise would be.

Practice: The Key to
Staying Sharp

GETTING INTO IT

You can work on your stance and swing at home or at a park or anyplace else there's room enough to swing a bat. A large rock or a newspaper can serve as home plate, or you can cut a home plate out of cardboard and put that down in front of you. Work on getting into your stance, bending forward first, and then softening the knees. Put your bat into position and get some kind of rhythm going. Check yourself by running over the specific stance points in your mind, or, better still, have your friend stand back and analyze you. Compare your stance with the photos in this book. And so forth. Then swing in slow motion and do the same thing.

What I'm saying is let yourself really *get into it*. Think about it. Analyze it. Spend some time getting your body into position and then concentrate on how it feels. Practice walking up to the "plate" and taking your stance time and again until you go into the right position and make the right moves almost automatically. Then do the same thing with your stride and swing. You're trying to establish good habits here, and as everyone knows, the only way to do that is through repetition.

THE BATTING TEE

Once the Absolutes are beginning to feel more comfortable, it's a good idea to begin working with a batting tee. As most ballplayers know, this is a telescoping, adjustable rubber-tube assembly attached to a wide rubber plate. The plate sits on the ground and a ball is placed on the end of the tube, which holds it at the desired height. Batting tees aren't too expensive. You can usually find a pretty good one for about twenty or thirty dollars.

But properly used, they're worth their weight in gold. All you need is a tee, a ball or two, and a fence to hit into. Set the tee so that the ball's at about waist level—that is, in the middle of your strike zone. Then take your position so that the ball is right where it should be at the point of contact if someone were pitching you strikes. Get into your stance and get your rhythm going. Then stride and swing just as you would in batting practice.

This is good practice by itself. But you can make it even better by attaching a piece of cardboard to the fence to serve as a target. Use a piece about four inches wide and seven inches long and put the tee fifteen or twenty feet away. With the target aligned with the ball at line-drive height, you ought to be able to hit it once out of every five swings. As you get better, try to hit it two out of five times, and so on. To make it even more interesting, you could practice with a friend and see who hits the target more often. With or without competition, some major-league players use this same exercise regularly, not just at the beginning of the season, as some Little Leaguers do.

OTHER DRILLS

Another good drill is to have someone stand off to the side and toss baseballs into your line of fire. Take your stance and start your rhythm. Then have your friend toss in the first ball. This is a great drill because the element of fear is eliminated. You're free to concentrate on shifting your weight and taking a good swing. And you get instant feedback, since if you aren't shifting your weight correctly, you'll have a lot of trouble hitting the ball.

Batting practice, of course, is excellent. But as I've said, without strikes pitched by the coach, a pitching machine, or a really good fellow player, batting practice is considerably less beneficial than it should be. Still, since it gives you a chance to learn to hit the kind of pitching you'll probably face in competition, it can be valuable. It's just that unless you're seeing consistent strikes, batting practice is not the time to do intense developmental work on your form. For that, the other drills are generally better.

Finally, there's a drill that's one of the best I've ever found. It requires either the coach or a good player on the mound, and it works like this. The batter stands at the plate and shifts his weight as he swings his bat back and forth, taking swing after swing, almost like a horizontal pendulum. On one repetition, just as the hitter is bringing his bat back, the coach starts to throw, timing things so that the ball reaches the point of contact just as the bat does.

In other words, the pitcher keys his movements to the batter instead of the other way around. The batter is constantly in motion, and it's the pitcher's job to put the ball where it's supposed to be at the right time. This can also be done with a pitching machine by holding the ball and dropping it into the mechanism at the right moment.

This drill accomplishes a number of things. It makes the batter acutely aware of the importance of rhythm and what it should feel like, and since he's always moving, he can never get still and tight. The tension is gone and in its place is a smooth, graceful stroke, complete with a weight shift back and forward, back and forward.

PRACTICE RIGHT

These are some of the most effective drills I know for developing a good hitter. But whether you use these specific exercises or some variation of them, it's essential to practice the right way when you do them. Unfortunately, most people tend to practice what they already do well instead of working to correct the things they do wrong. And some, particularly younger players, don't really know what practice should consist of.

You can take Little League kids, for example, and say, "Now go over there and hit the ball off the tee and into the screen." They'll go over, take three swings, and come back saying, "Okay, I can do that. What next?" The only solution is for the coach to go over and lead them and maybe get a competition going.

Practice: The Key to Staying Sharp

But if the coach will also take a little time to teach them how to practice, what to strive for, and so forth, they'll eventually be able to do it on their own. It's a mistake to assume that a kid automatically knows how to practice, just as it's a mistake to assume he automatically knows the best way to swing a bat.

Whenever you practice—and it should be often—try to incorporate all of the Absolutes in your stance and swing. Always take plenty of time to prepare your stance and, if possible, have someone check you frequently to make sure you're doing it right. Work on making that proper stance a reflex action, but always go over it in your mind to make sure you haven't forgotten anything.

Whenever you swing, whether at a pitch, at a ball on a tee, or with no ball at all, try to make sure that you step to hit, that you get full extension, that you throw the bat head at the ball, that your head goes down when you swing, etc. I know it's quite a list. And I realize that the movement of the swing makes incorporating Absolutes more difficult than is the case in the stance.

So concentrate on only one or two things at a time. Work on watching the ball or your weight shift or your follow-through for several swings. Then focus on some other point for several more swings.

Be thorough and strive for some definite improvement, however small, in each point you select. But try to avoid overworking it. Everyone sooner or later gets to where any further work on a certain point at that particular time is useless. And some days you're just not going to be as good as others. So after you've worked on something for a while, move on to something else, even if you haven't made any improvement. You can always go back to it later.

Regardless of the specific points you're working on, however, it's important to remember that nearly all the elements of good mechanics are intimately related. Each element makes some other element or elements possible. So even though you concentrate on different things at different times, do your best to incorporate all the Absolutes each time you swing. That way each element will come easier, and you'll be learning it not as something separate and distinct, but as something that is part of the whole process of swinging and hitting.

HITTING .300

From the time baseball began, a .300 average has been the benchmark by which a player's success at the plate has been judged. The .300 hitter is a star, the .240 hitter or the .250 hitter, a "failure." Yet statistically, there's not that much difference between them.

Look at it for a moment. The difference between a .250 hitter and a .300 hitter in 100 at-bats is *five* hits. That's all. Five more hits out of 300 swings or 100 at-bats, and you can raise your average 50 points. Hitting

consistently is still the most difficult feat in all sports. But at the same time, you've also got an awful lot of leeway to be successful if you maintain a sound, common sense approach to the problem.

The Absolutes are the essence of that approach. Good hitters have been showing us for years what you've got to do to be successful at home plate. The Absolutes are not theory or blindly accepted rules of thumb. They are proven fact, demonstrated by every successful batter from the beginning of the game to the present day.

But the Absolutes are more than a collection of techniques. Each is in some way related to, dependent upon, or complementary to the others. A balanced stance gives you a good base, but it also helps reduce fear and tension and makes it easier to stride with your front toe closed. Rhythm and movement in the stance eliminate tension and make it easier to stride, too, while also improving your weight shift and helping you make a positive, aggressive motion toward the pitcher. Striding with your front toe closed makes it easier to put your head down when you swing so that you'll see the ball. But to do that successfully, you also have to reduce fear, which means you must be balanced and begin from a balanced, workable stance. And so on.

Everything is connected. Taken as a whole, the Absolutes are more than the sum of their parts. Together they form a dynamic synthesis that shows you how to hit a baseball, and hit it both hard and often. If you will follow them, if you will practice and work hard, you *will be* successful. You'll get those five extra hits per hundred at-bats. You won't ever go 0 for 4. And, given a little ability, you can hit .300.

It's there if you want it.

Practice: The Key to Staying Sharp

11
THE ABSOLUTES LIVE ON

In the winter of 1984, just prior to the beginning of spring training, Charley Lau passed away after a long illness. And yet he left baseball with a legacy that still lives on. In fact, his techniques of hitting have been adopted by many coaches and players, who teach them to succeeding generations of ballplayers, proving that the Absolutes of hitting that he codified are as vital today as when he was alive.

Tony LaRussa, manager of the Chicago White Sox, analyzed Mike Schmidt, Jack Clark, Dale Murphy, and Carlton Fisk in earlier chapters. In this chapter, he will analyze eight more players—Don Mattingly, Wade Boggs, Darrell Evans, Bill Buckner, Dave Winfield, Keith Hernandez, Harold Baines, and Rickey Henderson—with an eye toward the Absolutes they embody.

LARUSSA ON LAU

My first association with Charley Lau occurred in 1963 as teammates on the Kansas City Athletics. Charley was a backup catcher who was always

interested in talking baseball, especially hitting. We were together again in 1970 when he coached for the Oakland A's and I was a utility infielder. During the rest of the 1970s and early 1980s, our friendship grew, but instead of being teammates we became opponents. He was with Kansas City for six years and the New York Yankees for three years. All the while he was developing his hitting theories. In 1982 we got back together with the Chicago White Sox, where he coached for two years until he died.

Something Charley would never say himself, but I can, is that the proof of the effectiveness of his theories was his teams' remarkable winning records. For example, his teams qualified for post-season plays six of the last eight years that he coached. This was no coincidence. Charley's offenses always had a sound mechanical base and an understanding of how each hitter could be most productive.

Lately, some people want to label and dismiss Charley as the guy who taught hitting off the front foot and the soft single to the opposite field. This is wrong because it's inaccurate and incomplete. Weight shift and the other Absolutes of good hitting did apply to all hitters, but the emphasis would differ with each player, depending on his abilities. In fact, power, home runs, and run production were very much a part of Charley's coaching when the individual was capable. Charley was behind Reggie Jackson's finest year in 1980—a .300 average with 44 home runs and 111 RBIs. Another example is the work Charley and Carlton Fisk did in 1982 and 1983 to restructure Carlton's stroke. The object was to produce more power and the results were 26 home runs in 1983 and 37 in 1985. As a clincher, just consider George Brett developing into a plus .300 hitter who hit 30 home runs in 1985.

What you had was Charley seeking to make each hitter capable of winning a game in the best way that particular player could. With a guy who couldn't hit the ball consistently into the seats, Charley stressed hitting to all fields. But, all his hitters were conscious of the game situations and were asking themselves, "Where can I hurt the other team the most?"

It made for a production offense and Charley was the guiding force. He was also more than just a hitting coach. He knew the pitching and catching part of the game and, combined with his knowledge of the league's hitters, he really helped our defense.

Charley was intelligent and had an analytical mind. His personality was also part of his genius. He knew his hitters and was a master at prodding or patting them at the right time so that their frame of mind was right for hitting. Whether he was calling you "dummy" or "hitterish," it was fine because it was Charley.

The game of baseball goes on no matter who leaves it. But only a few men leave something that lives on after they're done. Charley is one of those men because of his contributions to hitting. He was a great friend. I think of him every day. Enjoy reading his stuff, "dummy," and you'll get "hitterish."

The Absolutes Live On

HITTER ANALYSIS

DON MATTINGLY
HEIGHT: 5 feet, 11 inches
WEIGHT: 185 pounds
AVERAGE (1985): .324

Although in the major leagues only two years, Don has already established himself as one of the finest, most consistent hitters around. He won the American League batting title in his first full year in the league, hitting .343 in 1984, while leading the league in hits and doubles as well.

There are two things about Don's swing that stand out. First, he makes a very positive, aggressive move back toward the pitcher. Second, he always stays in the hitting zone, hitting through the ball. He is able to do this for a relatively long period of time.

Don, like all good hitters, finishes very high, illustrating this very point. This high finish might well be attributed to his full extension and not a collapsed swing, since Don's is indicative of a swing that does not collapse through the hitting zone.

Don hits from a balanced, workable foundation. His weight is on the balls of his feet, not on his heels. Also, he moves around the plate a good deal to relieve tension. He hits off his front stiff leg at the moment of contact, as you can see in photo 11-9, and he lands with his front toe closed. His complete stride is picture perfect. He is a perfect example of striding to hit as opposed to striding and hitting at the same time, as you can see in photo 11-4.

Like most other good hitters, Don uses the whole field to hit in. For instance, though a left-handed hitter, he still has the power to reach the "green monster" in Fenway Park. Try to pitch him away, and he peppers the wall. Try to pitch him inside and he pulls the ball. It's no wonder he led the league in RBI in 1985 with 145 and was named the league's MVP.

In photos 11-9 through 11-12, you'll notice how his head is still down and through the ball. He's following the ball, always finishing high. Though not one of the Absolutes, Charley would always tell players to finish high. The reason he stressed this was that there used to be a misleading phrase that was prevalent in baseball circles: you should always hit up on the ball. Charley felt that this was the wrong phrase, the wrong image to put into the batters' mind. Instead, he used to tell batters to finish high. This cleared their mind when swinging at the ball and kept them from dropping the rear shoulder too much. When a pitch is traveling ninety miles per hour, you don't have time to think about a lot of things. You have to react. However, once you start the swing—thought-free—there is time in the follow-through to concentrate on the "high finish."

HITTER ANALYSIS

WADE BOGGS
HEIGHT: 6 feet, 2 inches
WEIGHT: 190 pounds
AVERAGE (1985): .368

Wade, the 1985 American League batting champion, has hit better than .300 every year in pro ball since 1976, when he was with Elmira in the minor leagues. Along with Jim Rice and Johnny Pesky, he is the only Red Sox player to have 200 hits in two different seasons, and he holds the American League record for a rookie with a .349 average in 1982.

Wade is well known for staging hitting clinics during ball games.

Wade has a great stance, balanced and workable. His feet are shoulder's-width apart, which affords him maximum balance. He bends from the waist first, then the knees. He has a very good rhythm, rocking back and forth to give himself a good weight shift. His head is cocked upright to look directly at the pitcher, which is of great importance in order to see the ball from the moment it is released from the pitcher's hand.

Another thing to note about Wade's swing is his perfect execution of the stride. He steps to hit, not stepping and hitting at the same time (11-15) and he shows perfect balance, hitting off his stiff front leg, as you can see in photo 11-20.

Though his ritual of eating chicken before every game has received a lot of publicity, he's always credited both Ted Williams, early on in his career, and Charley, in the later period, with helping him develop his batting style and hitting technique. Wade is a fantastic worker, obsessed with hitting, always looking for a way to improve.

Essentially, Wade has a swing that does not produce the long ball, even though he is a very strong individual. Like all high-average hitters, he uses the entire field to hit in. He bounces the ball off the Fenway Park "green monster" when he's pitched away—he has the strength to hit it that far, and to hit it hard enough to get it off the wall. But pitch him tight with off-speed deliveries and he'll pull the ball. Either way, he's a real tough out, as his high career average of .351 proves.

Wade has a very compact and effective swing. He never fails to get that bat into the launching position when his front foot hits the ground. As you can see in this photo sequence, once the pitcher begins his motion, Wade drops his hands. But when his front foot hits the ground, he's got that bat in the launching position, which is just slightly below his shoulders. Now the bat is ready to go. His head goes down much as Steve Garvey's or Don Mattingly's does. He gets a full extension in his swing and finishes with his top hand off the bat. And yet this releasing of the top hand is unusual for Wade. This is the result of our camera's catching Wade hitting an off-speed pitch in which he was momentarily fooled, enough so that his swing is much earlier than usual. Ninety-nine times out of a hundred he will finish high, with both hands on the bat.

HITTER ANALYSIS

DARRELL EVANS
HEIGHT: 6 feet, 2 inches
WEIGHT: 205 pounds
AVERAGE (1985): .248

Darrell, who led the American League in home runs in 1985 with 40, reached double figures in round-trippers for the fifteenth consecutive year. Along with Hank Aaron and Davey Johnson, he made the 1973 Atlanta Braves the only team in history to have three 40 home-run hitters in one season.

This photo sequence of Darrell shows him hitting one out of the park in spring training. You'll notice that one of the Absolutes that Darrell illustrates most dramatically is keeping his head down when he swings. His head virtually burrows into the ball. Darrell's got his eyes directly in the hitting zone, and, as he swings, his head moves downward.

Darrell also illustrates another Absolute that Charley stressed, that is, a good weight shift from a firm rigid backside forward to hit from a firm rigid front side. In photo 11-25, you can see the perfect execution of his stride. He steps to hit, as opposed to stepping and hitting at the same time. In photo 11-26, you can see that his weight comes forward.

One of the misconceptions about hitting and the weight shift is that the eye, which can see only at ten frames per second, usually sees the recoiling action, that is, the batter in the follow-through position. Thus, many people believe that you have to stay back to hit a ball. But with a high-speed camera such as the one used here, you can see that Darrell's weight is actually over on the front and his back foot is off the ground. This means that his weight has shifted, much as a golfer's weight is shifted during his swing. You aren't able to see this with the naked eye because the human eye is not as fast as the lens of a camera.

In photo 11-31, you can see that Darrell's weight has moved forward as the ball is on the bat. Also notice that his top hand is underneath. He has great extension in his swing, hitting through the ball, which is one of the Absolutes.

HITTER ANALYSIS

BILL BUCKNER
HEIGHT: 6 feet, 1 inch
WEIGHT: 185 pounds
AVERAGE (1985): .299

A career .295 hitter, Bill has proved himself to be one of the most consistent hitters, first in the National League with the Dodgers and the Cubs and now in the American League with the Red Sox. Although he is not often thought of as a power hitter, Bill does get his share of RBI—110 in 1985. In fact, he's a clutch performer, as his team-leading .352 average with runners in scoring position in 1984 proves.

With the Red Sox for the past two years, Bill finds himself under the tutelage of batting coach Walt Hrniak, a Lau advocate, and Charley's influence is definitely apparent. As a matter of fact, Walt has mentioned Bill as one of the players on the team who best illustrates the Absolutes.

At the age of thirty-five Bill, one of the hardest working hitters in the league, decided to make some changes, some adjustments in his swing, all of them directly attributable to Charley's teachings. He developed a weight shift back before going forward, which allowed him to use the lower half of his body as well as the upper. He also moved off the plate somewhat and used his top hand less, releasing it after contact for more extension in his swing.

In studying Bill's swing, you'll always notice that his bat is in the launching position when his lead foot hits the ground. He's also got that all-important positive, aggressive motion back toward the pitcher.

In this photograph you·can see that Bill's head goes down into the hitting position when he swings. The bat is just about on the ball and Bill is getting full extension into his swing.

Another important factor in Bill's success as a hitter is that he always uses the whole field to hit in. He's got the ability to spray the ball around. Though a left-handed hitter, he can still bounce the ball off that "green monster" in Fenway.

HITTER ANALYSIS

DAVE WINFIELD
HEIGHT: 6 feet, 6 inches
WEIGHT: 220 pounds
AVERAGE (1985): .275

When Dave first joined the Yankees in 1981, Charley was still with the team. At that time, pitchers were trying to go in on Dave, trying to jam him a lot. Charley tried to help him by getting him off the plate. Today, you'll notice that Dave has taken that advice.

Incidentally, Charley felt that most great hitters would probably only

Dave has a big swing and he likes to go out after the ball. If you take a look at the photo sequence, you'll see that he makes a big move toward the ball, definitely scoring high in terms of his positive, aggressive move toward the pitcher. Dave really goes after the pitch. He has a very pronounced weight shift. His weight really rocks over onto his front foot. He also has full extension, and this is one thing that Charley always felt was a big part of the perfect swing.

get anywhere from twenty to twenty-five perfect swings throughout the course of a season, and these swings would not necessarily result in home runs. Instead, they might be perfect swings wherein the batter meets the ball and hits it solidly for a line drive. This doesn't mean that the batters weren't getting hits off slightly imperfect swings, but rather that these twenty to twenty-five ideal swings occurred when everything, all the Absolutes, was put together in perfect harmony.

Another of the Absolutes that Dave demonstrates so well is his willingness to use the entire field to hit in. Dave is known for his ability to spray the ball around, as well as being able to hit with power to the opposite field. His career average of .288 and the fact that he's been an All-Star for nine consecutive years certainly attest to that.

Dave also demonstrates both rhythm and movement in his stance. He has a very tension-free swing. Just prior to hitting he takes a step back with his front toe in order to shift his weight back just before he moves forward into the ball. When he does make contact, that front leg is stiff. In photos 11-47 through 11-49, you'll notice that he does allow his top hand to come off the bat very quickly after the swing. This is the result of Dave's full extension. This is something that Charley tried to teach in order to show that it was full extension that drove the ball the hardest.

HITTER ANALYSIS

KEITH HERNANDEZ
HEIGHT: 6 feet
WEIGHT: 195 pounds
AVERAGE (1985): .309

     In the middle of the 1985 season, Keith was mired in an uncharacteristic batting slump. He wasn't stroking the ball well, so the hits just weren't coming. His father, while watching some of the Met games off a satellite dish, noticed that from the center-field camera shot he couldn't see Keith's number when his son was at the plate. This meant that Keith's stance was too

You can see in this photo sequence that he keeps his head down and his eye on the ball as well as anyone. Also, his bat is always in the launching position at the moment his front foot hits the ground, even though his preparation is somewhat idiosyncratic previous to this. Just before the pitcher goes into his motion, Keith starts to move, bringing his hands in, and when his right foot hits the ground, he's in the perfect launching position, just like any other good hitter.

11-50

11-51

11-52

11-53

11-57

11-58

11-59

11-60

open, that he was leaving the hitting zone and setting up differently from previous years. Once his father pointed this out to Keith, he made the proper adjustment and finished out the year with a flourish, hitting .309 and knocking in 91 runs.

Keith, a career .301 hitter, demonstrates many of the Absolutes quite well. He has outstanding mechanics. His stance, with his feet square and shoulder's-width apart and his weight on the balls of his feet, is tremendous.

Keith is also very adept at using the whole field to hit in. He never limits himself to pulling the ball, but instead goes the way the ball is pitched, spraying it to all fields.

You'll notice that Keith strides with his front foot toe closed, which in turn keeps the hips closed until he commits to swinging. He is in constant motion. He does little things: wiggles his legs back and forth, shifting his weight slightly, moving his hands and arms, not out of position but just to keep the tension from building. All this helps produce a tension-free, picture-perfect, rhythmic swing.

11-54   11-55   11-56

Once Keith launches into his swing, he bends first at the waist and then at the knees. He lands with his front toe closed and hits off that stiff front leg, as you can see in photo 11-61.

11-61

HITTER ANALYSIS

HAROLD BAINES
HEIGHT: 6 feet, 2 inches
WEIGHT: 189 pounds
AVERAGE (1985): .309

Ted Williams once characterized Harold as perhaps the best young hitter in baseball today. Charley Lau thought much the same. Over the past few years Harold has proved them right, not only as a pure hitter but also as one who comes through in the clutch. In fact, he was one of the league leaders in game-winning hits in 1984 with 17, and he has a career average of .285.

Harold gets a lot of rhythm and movement into his swing, and he has good preparation motion. He will drop his hands before the pitch, but he always manages to get the bat up into the launching position very quickly. He also has tremendous weight shift.

The idea of a player's actually seeing the ball hit the bat is still a controversial area. A definitive scientific determination has not yet been made, but you can see that Harold's head does go down as he tries to see the ball hit the bat. The result? He does see the ball as far as he can. And yet, those eyes in photo 11-69 are focused slightly in front of the plate, out toward the pitcher, and not right on the ball.

Looking at the photo sequence, you'll see that when he gets his weight over to the front side, his back foot comes off the ground. In photos 11-68 through 11-73, you'll see how that back foot is coming off and how rigid his front side is. He hits from a firm back side to a rigid front side.

Harold also has tremendous extension. Notice how his top hand leaves the bat after making contact and then rolls over the bottom hand. This isn't an Absolute, but Charley always talked about that top hand having to be on the underside of the bat through the hitting zone. Looking at Harold, you can see just what Charley was talking about.

Another interesting thing to note is the matter of whether or not the batter actually sees the ball hit the bat. Check the eyes in photos 11-68 and 11-69 and you'll see that Harold's are focused somewhere in front of the plate, but not directly on the ball. Charley tried to get players to actually see the ball hit the bat, but this confirms the fact that peripheral vision is very much involved in hitting a baseball. Some coaches believe that the actual hitting of the ball might be done more by kinesthetic feel (or some action where the player is calculating the flight of the ball) of where it will wind up when it will make contact with the bat.

HITTER ANALYSIS

RICKEY HENDERSON
HEIGHT: 5 feet, 10 inches
WEIGHT: 195 pounds
AVERAGE (1985): .314

As the only player in baseball history ever to steal over 100 bases in three different seasons, naturally Rickey is known primarily for his speed and base running. And yet he is also a fine hitter, having only twice since 1976, the year he entered the major leagues with Oakland, hit under .290. In 1985, his first season in a Yankee uniform, Rickey had an especially good year, getting close to the career high average he had as an Oakland A in 1981 when he hit .319.

The photograph shows Rickey in his follow-through. Though this shot doesn't really do Rickey's extension justice, you can still get some idea of just how far out he goes. You can also see that his left hand is still on the bat while his right has been released, and that he lands with that front toe closed.

Rickey has a unique stance. He gets into a very low crouch, which enables him to go from back to forward, as Charley used to say. In other words, he is able to get that good weight transfer by putting himself into that low crouch.

Another of the Absolutes that Rickey illustrates well is that he always makes a very positive, aggressive motion back toward the pitcher. He is also another good example of a player who is able to use the entire field to hit in, going the way the ball is pitched, spraying his hits to left, right, or center.

INDEX

CHARLEY LAU studied the art of hitting for his entire professional career. As a journeyman catcher for Detroit and later for Baltimore he had a unique vantage point for observing just what it is that makes some batters successful while others of equal or greater ability go hitless game after game. His observations led to questions—many of which had never been asked before—about hitting, about how to maximize your power, and about many of the old rules of thumb everyone had always accepted as given.

Taking full advantage of the latest videotape and photographic technology, Charley Lau vigorously pursued the answers to these questions, spent countless hours experimenting with different techniques, and analyzed the hitting styles of hundreds of batters. Gradually, he realized the mechanics and keys of good hitting and his system of teaching evolved.

A natural teacher, Charley Lau used his knowledge to improve the batting averages of the Orioles, the A's, the Royals and the Yankees. And through his work with individual players, such as Hal McRae and George Brett, he earned a reputation as one of the most respected and effective hitting instructors in the game. Few people knew more about hitting than Charley Lau, and no one was better qualified to show you how to become a consistent hitter. Charley Lau passed away in 1984.

ALFRED GLOSSBRENNER is a freelance writer and editor whose previous books have covered a variety of subjects, including men's gymnastics, women's track and field, and trampolining. He lives in Yardley, Pennsylvania.

TONY LARUSSA is manager of the Chicago White Sox. He worked with Charley Lau for years and is an expert on the Lau method.